AN
INFANTRYMAN'S STORIES
FOR HIS DAUGHTER

AN INFANTRYMAN'S STORIES FOR HIS DAUGHTER

Lieutenant Colonel (Ret) James M. Tucker

with

Lieutenant Colonel (Ret) John E. Gross

iUniverse, Inc.
Bloomington

An Infantryman's Stories For His Daughter

iUniverse books may be ordered through booksellers or by contacting:

iUniverse
1663 Liberty Drive
Bloomington, IN 47403
www.iuniverse.com
1-800-Authors (1-800-288-4677)

ISBN: 978-1-4620-4203-6 (sc)
ISBN: 978-1-4620-4204-3 (ebk)

Printed in the United States of America

iUniverse rev. date: 11/09/2011

CONTENTS

BOOK ONE

BOOK TWO

BOOK ONE

PROLOGUE

Charlotte, this book is for you. In case some other person may wonder why I put this book together, I'll explain. In April of 2009, I decided to attend the 90th reunion of the officers who had been in combat with the First Infantry Division, "The Big Red One". The first such reunion I attended was at the Waldorf Hotel in New York in 1969, following a year in Vietnam as an executive officer and operations officer of an Infantry battalion in the First Division. I assumed, because of my age, that the 2009 reunion would probably be my last. While I was making plans I came to realize that because of the physical demands of the trip, it would be impossible for me to attend without someone to assist me. I decided to ask you to accompany me as my *aide-de-camp*. You had never been to Washington, D.C. and I thought you would enjoy the trip.

As the reunion trip unfolded, you made what to me was a startling statement, "Daddy, I don't know anything about your military career." Only then did it come to me that you had not been born until I was a Lieutenant Colonel and that you had been too young to remember any of my assignments except my last, as an instructor at the Air Ground Operations School at Hurlburt Field, FL.

Your comment started me thinking about what my family had missed as I traveled around the United States, Europe, the Middle East, and Asia. I served for 22 years, five of which were with the Ranger Department of the U.S. Army Infantry School. I spent two and a half years as an instructor at the Mountain Ranger Camp in Dahlonega, GA, two years as commander of the Florida Ranger Camp at Eglin AFB, Fl, and the remainder at the Department Headquarters at Fort Benning, GA. In 2008, I was inducted as a Distinguished Member of the Ranger Training Brigade in the Ranger

Hall of Fame. At the ceremony at Fort Benning, you, your mother, my sister, two nieces and my daughter-in law attended. Other than being proud and delighted that my family was able to attend the ceremony, I gave little thought to the fact they knew hardly anything about what I had actually done in the Army. Your comment at the reunion stayed with me and began to haunt me. I realized that I did not want to leave the earth without passing on to my family something that hints at the essence of whom I was as an Infantry soldier.

I decided to write three episodes from my service which, I hoped, would give my family insight into what made me what I am.

I asked John Gross, a retired Lieutenant Colonel of Infantry, who was one of my captains when I commanded the Florida Ranger Camp, if he would help me edit and assemble the three vignettes.

He agreed and as we got into the process, John said, "You know, you are being short sighted on this project." John recommended that I expand the short stories into a sort of memoir. He said, "If you want to leave your daughter the story of your army career, why not go all the way and tell it all?" John recommended I recount one or more episodes from each of my assignments. He also thought that there were too many great stories from my days as commander of the Florida Ranger Camp to leave out.

John said, "Let me canvass some of the guys we served with for their remembrances of the great times we had at the Ranger camp." John recommended that the book have two parts: first, stories from my different assignments written by me, and second, stories from the guys I commanded written by him. John had written a novel and a book of poems and knew the process of having a book published, so I agreed.

The result is a mixture of the serious, the sad, the melancholy, the ironic, the amusing, and the down right hilarious episodes that made up my Army career.

Charlotte, I dedicate this little book to you in response to your statement, "Daddy, I know nothing about your Army career."

I also dedicate it to Lorraine, my dear wife of 52 years, with love, respect, and appreciation for the support she gave me while I served, and for holding the family together during my absences. I also dedicate it to the memory of Carlton.

CHAPTER 1

THE RANGER CURSE

There seems to be two types of Infantry soldiers who wear the Ranger Tab. The first type goes through Ranger school, graduates, and then simply goes on with his career. Although this type of soldier is proud of his black and yellow tab, being a Ranger is not the central focus of who he is. He may be more proud of being a good staff officer, briefer, or instructor than he is of being a Ranger. To him, the Ranger tab is just another qualification badge.

The second type is one who lives the Ranger Creed. He takes the mission of the Ranger course seriously—to return to his home unit and elevate the level of training by passing on leadership techniques he learned in Ranger school. This type of Ranger tries at every opportunity to command Infantry soldiers and to serve with the Airborne, the 75th Ranger Regiment, the Ranger Training Brigade, or Special Forces. To this type of soldier, being a Ranger is the essence of who he is.

The Ranger attitude can certainly be a blessing. Being a hard-charging Ranger during one's entire career can take a soldier to the highest levels of Army leadership. For example, Hugh Shelton, the Chairman of the Joint Chiefs of Staff under President Clinton was one of my captains at the Florida Ranger Camp. Throughout his entire career, he lived the Ranger Creed. Also, all one has to do is to look at the uniforms of the current top leaders in the Army to see that they all wear Ranger tabs.

But the Ranger attitude can also have a dark side, and can even be a curse. In the Broadway play "Oklahoma", there is a little song with the words, "Everything you can do, I can do better, I can do anything better than you." A soldier who wears the Ranger tab and maintains himself in top physical condition, who studies and remains current in the art of war, and who has the attitude that nothing can stop him in his pursuit of excellence, might as well go around singing this little song.

A line from the Ranger Creed, states, "Acknowledging the fact that a Ranger is a more elite soldier who arrives at the cutting edge of battle by land, sea, or air, I accept the fact that as a Ranger my country expects me to move further, faster and fight harder than any other soldier."

In staff, recruiting, instructional or advisory assignments, one of which every officer must endure sometime during his career, this attitude can rub fellow soldiers the wrong way. Often, officers who are less fit, less dedicated, and less able feel intimidated by the Ranger in the office. Jealousy, friction and conflict can often result. If the one who feels intimidated happens to be the boss, trouble can easily follow, setting up a situation where the non-Ranger boss feels that the hard-charging Ranger subordinate must be "brought down a notch".

I'll give you an example of the Ranger Curse in action. One of my best captains at the Ranger Camp had risen to the rank of Lieutenant Colonel and had been given command of a battalion. He never could figure out why he had such a hard time pleasing the brigade commander. It seemed he could never do anything right.

One day the brigade commander asked him, "Do you know who I am?"

My former captain, now battalion commander, answered, "Yes, sir, you are the brigade commander."

"But do you know who I am? Do you remember me from 1968?"

"No sir."

"You were my Ranger instructor in Florida. You graded me. In fact, you flunked me on a patrol. It was the only thing I have ever failed at."

Later, that brigade commander stood my former captain at attention in front of his desk as he called a friend in personnel management at the Pentagon.

"I want you to tell me how to write an efficiency report that is not derogatory, but will insure the man never gets promoted," he said into the phone.

Thus ended the career of an officer who would have been an outstanding general in our Army. The Ranger Curse had struck again.

The best description of the Ranger attitude I have read ironically was written by a Frenchman. Jean Larteguy, French commando, soldier, and journalist, author of *The Centurions,* about French paratroopers in Algeria, wrote:

"I'd like to have two armies—one for display, with lovely guns, tanks, little soldiers, staffs, distinguished and doddering generals, and dear little regimental officers, who would be deeply concerned over their general's bowel movements or their colonel's piles; an army that would be shown for a modest fee on every fairground in the country. The other would be the real one, composed entirely of young enthusiasts in camouflage uniforms, who would not be put on display, but from whom impossible efforts would be demanded and to whom all sorts of tricks would be taught. That's the army in which I should like to fight."

From the time my Ranger Tab was safety-pinned to my fatigues, I have tried to live the Ranger life. As you will see, I often suffered from the curse of simply being a Ranger.

CHAPTER 2

MY EARLY CAREER

During my 22 years of service, I received many awards, commendations, accolades, promotions, and rewards. I was also shot at and missed, shot and hit, and shot down. I was offered an Article 15 (non-judicial punishment), which I refused. I then demanded a court martial, which never happened. I was asked to resign my commission, which I also refused to do. Finally, I was allowed to retire in my own time, at my request, without ceremony. Throughout all of these ups and downs, I continued to love the Army, because I love Infantrymen.

There is no other service member of America's armed forces who is as unique as the Infantryman. An Infantry commander leads a true cross section of American society. If a commissioned officer is lucky enough to lead a platoon, or command a company or battalion, he will have been exposed to every facet of our society. In my opinion, the learning experience of the Infantry officer who serves in combat with his soldiers is fourfold that of the average Army leader.

My first step toward being a career soldier was graduating from the Citadel in 1956. Although I had pinned on the gold bars of a second lieutenant and crossed rifles insignia, I did not truly become an Infantryman until I had finished my initial training at the Infantry Officers' Basic Course, Ranger school, Airborne school, and the Jumpmaster course, all at Fort Benning, Georgia.

Sometime during all of this, I found time to marry Lorraine Kaye, and zip off to a honeymoon in Cuba (Fidel had not yet taken over. He was still hiding in the mountains).

Then, leaving my new bride, I was off to Korea for fourteen months as a platoon leader in A Company, First Battle Group, 32nd Infantry of the 7th Infantry Division, the Bayonet Division. This assignment gave me my first contact with the Infantry soldiers I would grow to love. The only other things worth mentioning about this tour was getting to see a foreign culture first hand, and freezing my extremities off during the brutal Korean winter.

After serving 10 months in Korea, I became eligible for some leave time. I arranged to meet Lorraine in Japan for some post-wedding bliss. While making plans for the trip, Lorraine decided to travel by ship. Crossing the Pacific Ocean on an ocean liner takes a long time. As I was to find out, it took longer than we both expected.

Lorraine has always had an effect on those she met, particularly men. Predictably, on the ship, she became a favorite of the male members of the crew. In fact, the captain invited her to his table for dinner almost every night. He did everything in his power to impress her.

One day he asked her, "Have you ever been to Hawaii?"

"No", answered your mother, "But I hope to someday."

"Well," said the captain, it's not too much out of our way. We'll just stop there for a day or two. We found out later that the captain was not the decision maker. The president of the shipping line was aboard, making his last Pacific crossing before he retired. He had ordered the captain to extend the voyage by three days for a port call in Honolulu. Lorraine was delighted and enjoyed herself greatly while the ship was docked in Hawaii. It never occurred to her that I had planned my leave around the date of her arrival in Japan and would be anxiously awaiting her arrival.

When I landed in Tokyo, I went straight to our hotel. I was beside myself with excitement on the day the ship was supposed to arrive. I waited at the dock for hours, and was finally told the ship was delayed.

"How long?" I asked. Nobody knew. They just knew the ship was going to be late. Communications in those days were not as reliable as they are today. I tried to be patient while waiting again the next day. Finally, on the third day, I went to Hickam Air Force Base. I was desperate to find out where the ship was. As luck would have it, I found a couple of pilots who needed some flying time. While Lorraine was being wined and dined on the ship, I was becoming frantic. It is not in me to sit and do nothing; I had to take action. I talked the pilots into taking me to sea to look for the ship. We flew out as far as fuel would allow, but saw nothing. Unknown to either pilot I had a plan. As crazy as it sounds now, my plan was to find the ship and parachute in front of it and hope they would pick me up. Passion has driven alpha males to some crazy things.

Finally, the ship came in and your mom bounced down the gang plank as happy as a frisky pup. All she said was, "What a wonderful trip!" After a late start, our vacation got off to a rousing beginning. Japan in the mid-fifties was a soldier's paradise. Lodging was inexpensive and food and drink were of the highest quality. I had never heard of Kobe beef. It quickly became our favorite Japanese food. Arguably, it was, and still is, the highest quality beef in the world.

Sitting atop a fine hotel drinking Asahi beer and eating *edamami* (boiled soy beans) was a new and exciting experience for a grunt like me.

Your mom had traveled far more than I and was years ahead of me in knowing proper manners and other cultures. She was ready and willing to experience anything Japanese. One of the most talked about sites for American soldiers was the Tokyo *Ansan*, a public bath house that, besides the *ofuro*, or bath, offered full body messages, facials, toe cleaning, and spine, leg and foot adjustments. We had learned that nudity was no big deal in Japan. Men and women both used the *Ansan* at the same time. The Japanese gave each other privacy simply by not looking at one another in the bath house. We were eager to experience this aspect of Japanese culture.

The Japanese are a homogeneous people. They are mostly about the same height and have roughly the same body build. Many American soldiers had used the bath house so the appearance of *gaijins* (foreigners) was nothing new to the Japanese. But they had never seen a body like Lorraine's. There was some privacy during massages, but when we stripped down and showered, a sudden silence descended on the room. Every eye in the place was locked on Lorraine. There was a sudden and total lapse of Japanese manners as men and women alike gaped at your Mom. Her shyness seemed to magnify their interest. When we entered the public part of the giant pool there was again a total hush. This was one of the most enjoyable experiences during our stay in Tokyo. We still laugh about the reaction of the Japanese to a beautiful, fully developed American female.

One of the reasons I chose Tokyo as a destination was because I wanted to practice judo at the *Kodokan* which is the judo center of the world. I was able to workout with and learn from tenth-degree black belts. This was before the martial arts boom, and at that time Tokyo was the only place where tenth-degree masters could be found. There were Frenchmen, Belgians, Australians and many others from around the world there to learn from the masters. I thought I was reasonability good but in front of these masters, my pride was totally deflated and my body battered.

During our time in Japan we visited Hokkaido and saw just how beautiful the land of the Rising Sun was. We saw and did many memorable things in Japan. One of the most enjoyable was biking around the base of Mount Fuji. When we returned to Tokyo, Lorraine flew out and I returned to Korea. Just before my departure, a cyclone swept over Japan and cleared out all the smog. A lasting memory of a wonderful time was being able to see Mount Fuji from the Tokyo airport.

When I returned to Korea I worked out at the judo center in Seoul and became close friends with a young Korean who was later to become a world champion. When he beat the Japanese champion, he became a national hero. He was six feet two and weighed 200 pounds or more. When he and I walked the streets of Seoul the Koreans would move to the side and bow to him. I never saw him again after I left Korea but I would have loved to walk down the street with him after he beat the Japanese and became world champion.

When I returned from Korea as a first lieutenant, I was delighted to be assigned to the Ranger Department of the U.S. Army Infantry School with duty at the Mountain Ranger Camp near Dahlonega, Georgia. There I instructed young soldiers in the finer points of mountaineering and combat operations in mountainous terrain. After serving in Korea and spending my first winter as a Mountain Ranger, I decided there are two places one does not want to be on any night between Thanksgiving and the middle of March—on the demilitarized zone in Korea and the back side of Hawk Mountain in north Georgia.

The assignment at the Mountain Ranger Camp remains notable for me because it is where your mother and I bought our first home. Your grandmother loaned us the money to buy a nifty new fifty-foot-by-ten-foot mobile home. For two and a half years, the trailer was our home. We were happy there with our boxer named Anna Maria Felidas Von de Ann, and a skunk named Wimpie. Near the end of that tour, your brother Carlton was born. Considering your mother's comfortable background, I thought it important that you know she was perfectly content living in a trailer.

You might wonder why we didn't just rent a house in Dahlonega. I'll tell you why. Prior to my assignment to the mountains, a Ranger instructor named Tony Herbert lived in Dahlonega. Since Ranger instructors spent more than half of our duty working at night, leaving our wives and children alone, we were all concerned about their safety. We came up with several different methods to make sure our homes were secure. To insure the safety of his home, Tony owned a pit bull, which took his security mission seriously. Tony had installed a heavy gauged wire fence with a "Beware of the Dog" sign posted on it. Nervous about what might happen, Mrs. Herbert had warned the mailman not to rattle the screen door. The postman ignored her advice and was quickly on the receiving end of a pit bull attack. The dog simply broke through the screen door and went after the hapless mail carrier. Since our boxer bore some resemblance to a pit bull, no one would rent us a house.

If you remember, you met Tony Herbert when I was inducted into the Ranger Hall of Fame as a Distinguished Member of the Ranger Training Regiment. Tony was not an average Infantryman. He had come out of Korea as the most highly decorated enlisted soldier who fought in that war. His exploits are covered in his book *Soldier*. He is one of the few officers to raise a red flag about our involvement in Vietnam. His book was critical of many aspects of the Vietnam War, and when it was published, the Army turned against him. Not only did he stand his ground against the Army, but he held up during a blistering interview on CBSs news magazine show, "60 Minutes". Tony retired as a lieutenant colonel, but should have been a general; he just refused to toe the line. His story would make a hell of a movie. The legacy he left at the Mountain Ranger camp was that no one would rent a house to a Ranger for many years. Throughout my life, I have feared no man, but there are two whom I would rather not get into a friendly fight with: Tony Herbert and Retired Major General Ken Leuer.

One of the things I enjoyed most about serving as a Ranger instructor was the mentoring young officers received from our seniors. One of the most inspiring and touching aspects of serving in the Infantry, and one that is rarely spoken or written about, is how senior officers take junior officers under their wings and give them the benefit of their experiences, wisdom and advice. During my Ranger assignments, I had the opportunity to learn from many truly outstanding Infantrymen, but few came close to

Colonel John T. Corley, at that time the Ranger Department Director. With two Distinguished Service Crosses, eight Silver Stars, two Legions of Merit, four Bronze Stars and the Purple Heart, he was one of the most highly decorated officers to serve in World War II and the Korean War. He served an Infantry Battalion commander in the Big Red One through much of World War II. When the Korean War started, he was asked for personally by General Douglas MacArthur. I did not know him well when I was a Ranger instructor, but I got to know him personally after his medical retirement. He had awarded me the Soldiers' Medal for entering a downed helicopter to help save the crew. In some of our conversations, I saw how the demons of past combat ate at his soul. During his last years he suffered greatly from what today would be called Post Traumatic Stress Disorder. He was one of the finest leaders I ever knew.

Colonel Corley left a legacy in the Army that will be difficult to equal. He made sure that the Ranger course would become a permanent part of Army training. Also, he rewrote the Army's physical training test, making sure that soldiers demonstrated the physical skills required on the battlefield. But his most lasting contribution was opening Ranger training to majors and lieutenant colonels. Many of this original group, including Sidney Berry, became generals. Berry was the senior major in the army when he went through the course, and became the first Ranger-qualified general. (Sidney was the one-star assistant commandant of the Infantry School when I commanded the Florida Ranger Camp. Later he would become the Commandant of West Point as a three-star.) Because of Corley's efforts, eventually, all West Point and Regular Army ROTC combat arms officers were required to attend Ranger School. This insured a continuing pool of hard-core leaders and future generals. A tribute to Colonel Corley's efforts is the fact that all of our top leadership in the today's Army wear Ranger Tabs. Colonel Corley was loved by his troops and feared by his peers and seniors. He was one hell of a soldier. He left his mark on many, many Infantrymen.

After I made captain, Lorraine and I traveled back to Fort Benning where I attended the Infantry Officers' Advanced Course, which was designed to prepare me for company command and service on battalion staff. I had been extremely happy up until this point in my career, since I had had only Infantry assignments. Upon graduation from the advanced course, however, I was broken hearted to learn that I was to be assigned to the Fourth Logistical Command in Verdun, France, as an assistant G-1 (personnel staff officer).

While stationed in Verdun, your mom and I had a great time. Since I was only a captain, military quarters were not available, so we had to live on the economy among the French people. The only place we could find to live was in an old building that had housed the headquarters of the Gestapo in World War II. It was a huge imposing three-story structure surrounded by a ten-foot tall steel fence. To me it seemed like a European castle. The gate to the city of Verdun was the famous towers which was the inspiration for the Army's Corps of Engineers insignia. The river Meuse formed a kind of moat on one side of the building.

The outside of the building might have looked like a castle, but your mother cried when she saw the stark austerity of the apartment inside. We had only three rooms and a kitchen. Even to an Infantryman from the red clay hills of Mississippi, it was a bare-bones existence. Your Mom set to work and soon the small apartment was a warm, livable home.

A concierge came with the apartment. Madam Everod tended the garden where she grew escargot, herbs, fruits and vegetables. This wonderful French lady immediately fell in love with Carlton, who returned her affection two fold. Lorraine could not cook on the 1900-era gas stove, so we hired a French lady named Julia to prepare our meals. Our daily meals consisted of fresh vegetables, meats and wine. Julia became our closest friend and she and her husband became Carlton's god parents. Carlton actually learned French and translated for us. What a wonderful gift Julia was to us.

Lorraine spoke with a deep-south accent that few French people had ever heard. They would often stop what they were doing and come close to her just to listen to her speak. Lorraine would gesticulate grandly while trying to find the proper words in her Mississippi-accented French. Of course French men in particular were fascinated by her.

The French officers' club was located about two hundred feet from where we lived. I hesitated to take Lorraine there because her southern charm was often mistaken by French officers as a sexy come-on. It was during this time that President DeGaulle was bringing the French army home from Algeria. Most of the returning officers were battle-hardened veterans from the French Foreign Legion. I was fascinated by many of their stories about combat in Algeria and Vietnam.

It was not uncommon for the foreign legion officers to get drunk and jump from the roof of their club into the Meuse River. The leap was about forty feet straight down, but they also had to jump ten to twelve feet horizontally to make the water. This required them to take a running start. Some unfortunates failed to reach the river and landed on the concrete sidewalk. With the state of morale in the French army at that time, I wondered if depression caused some of these officers to miss the river on purpose. Near the end of our tour, the club had erected a chain-link fence around the roof to stop the late-night leaps into the river.

The only bright spot in the 4th Log assignment was the opportunity to attend the British Commando School in Lymston, England. Staff work in the G-1 personnel office was mind-numbing, but it offered the advantage of having plenty of time to prepare for commando school. I spent the last six months of my Verdun assignment getting into top physical condition. My goal was to run 20 miles in four hours in combat boots. I accomplished that feat and actually went further—30 miles in seven hours. I thought I was completely prepared for the commando school. Boy, was I wrong!

My rude awakening came when I found out that the commandos did not run—they speed-walked. My running did not prepare me for walking at a blistering pace carrying a weapon and a heavy pack. I had never been physically punished as I was in commando school. When we moved in formation, we never ran, we speed-walked. The WW II U.S. Army Rangers were trained by British Commandos, so the tactics and techniques similar to our Ranger school offered no challenge. But the British NCOs particularly enjoyed punishing this Yank. After training during many evenings, the officers further punished me by drinking me to my knees and watching me crawl to the nearest place where I could throw up my guts. There is a stone bridge built by the Romans near a pub in Exeter that still has scratches caused by my fingernails while I was heaving. I tried to hide from my commando classmates while performing this humiliating act, but, alas, they knew all about it. There are great beer drinkers in all nationalities, but I will put the Brits up against all of them.

The final phase of commando training was an escape-and-evasion exercise. Simply stated, the object of this exercise was to out-smart and out-run the enemy forces that were out to catch the students. The exercise began with what was called the "wet stage". It crossed Exmoor, a swampy peat bog which was five miles across. Once the NCOs had speed-marched us through the wet phase, they turned us loose and we were on our own. That was my kind of challenge, 20 miles carrying full gear plus a Self-Loading Rifle (SLR) which weighed the same as our M-14 rifle. I finished the 20 miles in four hours, the best time ever, I was told. I was proud to receive the commando medal, but I never got a chance to get even with my drinking buddies.

When I was first assigned to the 4th Logistics Command, I voiced my displeasure to the chief of staff. I told him I needed to be commanding a rifle company. Rather than chewing me out for such a selfish and immature complaint, Brigadier General Joe Heiser had said, "Son, you work hard and do me a good job in G-1, and in a year, I will get you a company command in Germany." I did and he did.

True to his word, BG Heiser had me assigned as commander of C Company, 1st Battalion, 15th Infantry of the 3rd Infantry Division in Kitizen, Germany. Here, my love for the Infantry soldier grew as we trained and maintained to be ready to meet the Russians if they ever attacked West Germany. Near the end of this rewarding assignment, my company was selected to represent the 3rd Infantry Division which had liberated the City of Colmar, France from the Germans in WWII. It was here that a defining event in my career took place.

CHAPTER 3

THE COMMAND
THAT CANNOT BE GIVEN

As I was nearing the end of my command time, the battalion commander, Lieutenant Colonel Frank Phelps Jones said, "Tucker, you are to represent the division in a parade in France. Since you were assigned there, you are the most qualified for this job."

Most people might not believe it, but Infantry soldiers did not spend much time at drill and ceremonies. Training for combat and maintaining vehicles and equipment took up most of their time. As a result, we entered into three days of intense marching to prepare for the parade. One of the hardest requirements in drill is to maintain proper alignment while marching. My troops, who had not marched very much since basic training, worked and sweated until they could "dress to the right and cover down" very well at quick step.

One of the most difficult times to stay aligned in a parade is when the command "Eyes Right" is given. When the company approaches the reviewing stand, "Eyes Right" is the signal for all the soldiers in the formation (except for the file on the extreme right) to turn their heads and eyes to the right where the reviewing stand is located. This movement is designed to honor the reviewing officer or dignitary. When "Eyes Right" is commanded, the company officers render the hand salute and the company guidon is dropped from the vertical to the horizontal position. If this movement is not rehearsed over and over, the formation has a tendency to drift to the right at exactly the wrong moment. After passing the reviewing stand, the command "Ready, Front" returns the troops' heads and eyes back to the front. We rehearsed "Eyes Right" time after time until we could do it perfectly.

The trip to Colmar was a treat for the soldiers. When we arrived, we were greeted by members of the French army and were provided with an interpreter. Before the parade, we were given time to walk the streets and enjoy the festivities.

Perhaps no leader of an allied country had been as difficult to deal with as Charles DeGaulle. From the early days of WW II, when the Germans invaded France and many "Free French" escaped the country, DeGaulle acted as if he were the actual leader of France instead of an exile. On the eve of the Normandy Invasion, General Eisenhower asked DeGaulle to radio a speech to his countrymen asking them to rally to the allies. DeGaulle refused. He said he would be willing to ask the French citizenry to rally to him instead. DeGaulle had a history of doing things his way. He remained a thorn in the side of the allies throughout the war and afterward.

As the bands began to play, my company was ushered to our position in the lineup. All of a sudden, my battalion commander ran up and said, "Tucker, there has been a change in the location of the reviewing stand. General DeGaulle will be on the left side of the street. Why was the reviewing stand suddenly on the other side of the street? Because that is where General DeGaulle wanted it.

I was too shocked to respond with any comment other than, "Yes, Sir!" I asked myself, "Do we do 'Eyes Left'?"

I suddenly realized that all the rehearsals we had done were for naught. The right file, which was to look straight ahead to keep the company going straight, now had to look to the left—and the left file, which had never practiced the movement, would have to keep its head and eyes to the front. The reality of the "Eyes Left" command was equally devastating to my guidon bearer, platoon leaders, NCOs and soldiers. Never in my years of marching at the Citadel or in the Army had I heard the command "Eyes Left." There is no such command in the Army Field Manual 22-5, Drill and Ceremonies.

Frantically, I tried to communicate what was about to happen to over 100 soldiers as the bands drowned out my instructions. What we were about to do was dumbfounding. As I ordered, "Forward, March", I felt like the Infantry soldiers of WWI must have felt when the order was given to go "over the top"—that survival was not an option. Much of what happened next is blurred in my memory. One reason I don't remember much is the fact that I was marching in front of the company and could not see what was going on behind me. I imagined that when I shouted, "Eyes. Left" the company simply fell apart.

Years later, Lorraine found a picture of me marching and saluting in front of my company as we passed the reviewing stand. The color guard and I were the only ones visible in the photograph. God only knows what the company formation behind me looked like.

I vividly recall General DeGaulle standing straight and tall, peering down that great nose of his at what must have been the worst alignment of a parade formation he had ever witnessed.

After we finished the parade in a park, the entire company was invited to lunch at a French mess hall. As the party progressed, I happened to see a television set playing at the front of the room. General DeGaulle was speaking and I asked our French liaison officer what he was saying. He casually replied that the general was stating that all American troops had to leave France.

Historians will say that DeGaulle's decision to evict American troops from France had been in the works for some time. But I know the real story. DeGaulle kicked American troops out of France because he was so disgusted by my company's sloppy "Eyes Left", the command that cannot be given. To this day I know that it doesn't take a president or secretary of state to get our Army kicked out of a country; it just takes an Infantry captain.

CHAPTER 4

NOTIFICATION OFFICER

After my "Eyes Left" performance in front of Gen. Degaulle, the Army must have considered me toxic for further use in Europe. Not everyone has the opportunity to profoundly shift international relations with a single command!

I was next assigned to Middle Tennessee State University as an instructor in the Reserve Officers Training Corps (ROTC) program. Such an assignment was part of every officer's career building during those years. It provided a wonderful opportunity to enhance an officer's education as he continued to develop his leadership skills. In the ROTC program, we taught the basics of leadership and tactics and were able to inspire future officers to be the best they could be.

As one of my mentors pointed out to me, a truly professional officer, when not serving in combat, is either in command, in school, or instructing. I tried to meet those requirements throughout my career.

During this time (1965-1967) the Vietnam War was growing hotter. The reality of war hit home when I learned my platoon sergeant at the Citadel, Terry Cordell, had been killed in action. He was the first Citadel cadet graduate to die in Vietnam. As I went about my instructional duties, I kept an eye on what was happening in Vietnam and I read widely about the conflict. As I read Roger Triquier's *Modern Warfare,* I had a difficult time understanding his description of the French view of counterinsurgency. As I watched the war on the evening news, it resembled WWII and Korea. I still had a lot to learn.

One of the additional duties assigned to ROTC instructors was that of "notification officer". What the notification officer had to do was go to the home of the next of kin of the deceased soldier and tell the family that their loved one had been killed in action.

This task was assigned on a rotational basis by use of a duty roster, and in the spring of 1967 my turn came. The officer who had been killed was a ROTC Distinguished Military Graduate from MTSU. He had been in Vietnam for six months when he died.

An NCO accompanied me as I arrived at the house with the telegram. As I stood on the front porch, I could see a young woman and an older lady through the dining room blinds. The young woman was standing on the dining room table and the older lady was sitting in a chair hemming her dress. When I rang the doorbell, a man answered.

The only thing I remember was the young woman saying that she was getting ready to join her husband in Hawaii for his R&R. After that, my memory shut down. I don't remember any of the conversation that took place after that. It was probably my brain activating some defense mechanism to keep me from going into shock.

My experience was not as bad as what some of my fellow officers had endured. Some of them told me horror stories about notifications. When I went home that night, I vowed I would never go through that experience again. Notification duty is the most horrible assignment an officer can perform. It goes on today as it did then. My prayers are that it will go away soon.

I have never been shy about asking for favors from senior officers. Within the next few days I found the phone number for Lieutenant General Albert O' Conner, who was the U.S. Army Deputy Chief of Staff for Personnel. He had been the commanding general of the 3rd Infantry Division when I was stationed in Germany. He had apparently forgotten the Colmar "Eyes Left" parade, but he did remember me.

The favor I asked him for was an immediate assignment to Vietnam—I did not intend to stay at MTSU and be a notification officer again. His only question was "Are you sure?" My answer was an emphatic "Yes, Sir!" He said, "You will have orders next week." LTG O'Conner was aware that LTC Richard Cavazos was being assigned as commander of the 1st Battalion, 18th Infantry of the Big Red One. He gave me one of the biggest professional favors anyone has given me in my career. He gave me a direct assignment to the 1st of the 18th. That assignment changed my life forever

CHAPTER 5

TO VIETNAM
WITH THE BIG RED ONE

One of my pet sayings has always been, "I don't want to get ambushed!" Whether in a social setting, the office, training in the field, or in combat, I did not want to be surprised, or ambushed. This deeply felt objective might never have been a part of my life if I had had a different experience in Vietnam. Fate was with me.

My arrival in Vietnam was unlike that of most officers I know of. Usually arrivals went like this: After landing at Bien Hoa airbase in Vietnam, soldiers were bussed through town to the 90th Replacement Company on the adjoining Long Binh compound. There, they waited until transportation was announced which would take them to the divisions where they would be assigned. Soldiers then went by bus, truck, helicopter or C-130 to their respective units.

When arriving at their divisions, enlisted soldiers went to the division replacement depot where they would await their assignments to units. Infantry officers reported to the division personnel officer (G-1) who would tell them which battalion they would be assigned to. Then, officers would undergo a week of "jungle training" designed to teach them what they needed to know to operate in Vietnam. Finally, new officers would fly out to their battalions to begin work.

Most every officer going to Vietnam went through this process—except me. Direct assignment to a particular battalion was unheard of. But my assignment was arranged so that I reported directly to the 1st Battalion, 18th Infantry. I skipped the in-processing at the 90th Replacement Company and the G-1 at the First Infantry Division. I simply caught a helicopter and flew out to the battalion. If this had not happened to me, there is no telling how my life would have been different.

Some say marriage is the supreme life changing event in one's life. Combat is even more life changing. My existence was never the same after meeting LTC Richard Cavazos (The Boss). His first words to me were, "If you make it as my executive officer, I will make you my S-3." I did not fully appreciate the meaning of those words until weeks later.

I had never been around many Hispanic men, let alone officers, but I had no reservations about serving under LTC Cavazos. The only minority officers I had ever had contact with were African American, and I never had any problem serving with them. Race meant nothing to me. My mother always reminded me that neither race nor riches makes the man—character does. I once asked my mother how it was possible for me to have been raised in the redneck south without any racial bias whatsoever.

She said, "Because you grew up in Yocona, Mississippi and we all were poor. Color never mattered. The only thing that was important was putting food on the table."

She also reminded me that when I was a baby, my wet nurse was a black woman who lived on a farm across the road. There was no refrigeration or bottle formula in our world.

I arrived at the 1-18 Infantry ready to see if I could make it as a soldier. After all my years of training, I wondered how I would react when the first bullet cracked overhead. Infantrymen throughout history have asked themselves the same questions as they went into combat for the first time. Will I make it? Will I hesitate? Will I freeze? Will I do my duty? Will I let the soldiers down? I was confident, but like all Infantrymen before me, I was not certain.

As I said, I sometimes wonder what my life would have been like if I had gone through the normal assignment process and ended up serving in another battalion, under another battalion commander. Pure luck placed me with the best battalion commander who ever served in Vietnam.

My initial assignment was as the executive officer (XO). In a battalion consisting of as many as 750 soldiers, the commander cannot possibly do everything by himself. He has a staff to help him with the avalanche of details, paperwork, and coordination required by the Army. The XO's job is to supervise the staff, which consisted of the S-1 or personnel officer, the S-2 or intelligence officer, the S-3 or operations officer, and the S-4 or supply officer. In combat, the most important staff officer is the S-3, who is responsible for planning every movement the battalion makes. My job as XO was to insure the staff provided the soldiers everything they needed at all times.

When I arrived, the rainy season was in full swing and the Viet Cong, "Charlie" as he was called by U.S. soldiers, was selective in his attacks against our night defensive positions (NDPs). Each Infantry battalion had a base camp (known as "the rear") from which it operated. I spent much of my time back at the base camp making sure the rifle companies were fully provided for.

After a month or so, the S-3, an experienced, battle-wise captain, got his rotation orders. By this time I felt comfortable with the Boss, and I believe he was comfortable with me. He knew I always put the soldiers first, particularly the lowest ranking "grunt".

It was at this time in my career that I developed a deep and abiding love for the lowest ranking soldiers, the ones who are seldom noticed or praised; the ones a commander must keep alive if he is to live to accomplish his mission. I underwent a gradual transformation as I watched the Boss fight battles and take care of the troops he loved. Without any realization or intent on his part he was altering the way I would be the rest of my life.

My first chance to see how I would react to the crack of the bullet came in July or August, 1967, when our night defensive perimeter (NDP) was attacked during a tropical monsoon rain. The rain came down so hard that it collapsed the roofs of many of the sandbag bunkers. No combat unit in the 1st Division was allowed to bed down without overhead cover consisting of sandbags. We used the dirt we dug out of our foxholes to fill the sandbags. For the frame to hold the sandbags over our foxholes, we used limbs and trunks from trees and bushes that we cut down as we cleared fields of fire. If any commander failed to make his unit dig in properly with overhead cover, he was immediately relieved of command. There was zero tolerance on this rule. On many occasions we had to dig in at night, so we fired artillery illumination rounds and had aircraft drop parachute flares so soldiers could see to build their overhead cover.

The preferred time of attack by the Viet Cong (VC) and North Vietnamese Army (NVA) was at night or during a driving rain storm.

Darkness and bad weather hampered our ability to use helicopter gunships and Air Force tactical air.

This particular attack began with our listening posts (two or three-man positions stationed 50 or so meters outside our perimeter) notifying us of movement around their positions. When that happened, we pulled the listening posts back inside the perimeter, went to 100% alert, prepared our artillery and mortars, and alerted helicopter gunships and Air Force tactical air support.

The Boss taught me that no matter what the nature of the conflict, artillery must be the predominant supporting fire. I am alive today because he taught me to keep our soldiers safe and let the artillery do the killing. The Boss's use of artillery was legendary in the Big Red One.

I once saw what happened to an artillery battalion commander who had failed to provide the Boss's requested fire immediately and on target. The Boss, who was the same rank as the artillery commander, had him brought to our command post by the division's commanding general. If front of the two-star division commander, the Boss said, "I want him fired!" From that point forward, my battalion always got all the artillery support requested. The fire came immediately and on target.

When a famous Infantry commander was taking over a new command, he asked only one question: "How good is my artillery?" To this day, when I join my fellow officers at our yearly gatherings, I always sit for a while with the artillerymen. No infantryman can survive long without the artillery. From my combat experience, I learned that big Air Force bombs and helicopter gunships are fine, but they cannot be relied on like the artillery. Only artillery can be called on quickly enough and close enough to save the Infantryman.

During my first battle, one of our listening post soldiers has hit either by a large caliber bullet or a rocket-propelled grenade. His shoulder was blown off. We got him to our aid station where our battalion surgeon (each battalion had a doctor assigned) tried to stop the bleeding. We immediately called for medical evacuation (Dust-Off), but were told the rain and the winds were too severe. I understood that fully. However during the back-and-forth over the radio, one of the senior aviators, either the commander or executive officer of the Dust-Off unit, intervened. He asked for volunteers to go with him to evacuate this soldier. He got a warrant officer for a co-pilot and a crew chief and took off. When we learned that there was a chance to get this soldier out, we were so elated that we temporarily forgot that we were being attacked by an enemy force that outnumbered us.

When the battle subsided a bit, we thought we heard an in-bound helicopter, but it never arrived. We were later notified that the Dust-Off helicopter had crashed and all aboard were killed. Those men gave their lives trying to save one of our soldiers, who unfortunately also died later that night. It was just a normal night in Vietnam. John Gross wrote a poem summing up what a normal night in Vietnam was like. I include it here because it describes the frustration we often felt.

A NORMAL NIGHT IN NAM by John Gross

We called the Binh Son "Mother", No compliment, understand.
It's where the French grew rubber, the rows of trees well-planned.
We were not allowed to damage those oozing trees, you know,
the economy demanded the piasters from the flow.

Old Charlie didn't notice or seem to place great stock
in whether pails of rubber ever made it to the dock.
You see, the groves protected, sheltered, shaded well and hid
all the bunkers, trails and meanness that the little bastards did.

They booby-trapped and ambushed, punji-staked and slinked away.
They mined and sniped and mortared almost every single day.
So we went in to find them, those silent, deadly foes;
to ambush the ambushers, to chase them from the groves.

Every afternoon at dusk, our guys would sally forth
at a careful, dragging shuffle, with their weapons at the port.
Their gear and guns were standard, the same stuff every night:
claymores, starlights and radios, our nation's awesome might.

Their mission was quite simple: lie beside plantation trails,
and blow away old Charlie, to soundly kick his tail.
As the sun went slowly down behind the steaming jungle hills,
Old Mother Binh Son swallowed them to test their soldier's skills.

I got a call at midnight, and not for idle chat.
Commo with the ambush had been cut off—just like that.
The 'bush had not been heard from for four hours and the worst
was certainly suspected judging from the captain's curse.

He said, "Go in and find them, take your whole platoon.
Don't come out until you find them, or until tomorrow noon.
After that we're pulling out, so find them fast. Oh, yes, be sure that you don't
shoot them up. It's dark in there, I guess."

I couldn't think about it very much and fill with doubt.
It was an urgent mission. We had to get them out.
Not a single shot was fired; not a single word was said.
We went about our business though our chests were filled with dread.

We squinted at the shadows. We listened for a call.
Was that a good or bad guy? Or was nothing there at all?
We crept the groves 'till daylight; soaked with sweat and filled with fear,
'til we got a call from Charlie Six: "You can come on in, they're here."

They had simply gone to sleep, turning off their radio.
They walked on in at daybreak, embarrassed heads were hanging low.
At first it made us angry to spend such a useless night.
To risk ourselves for sleepers didn't seem quite right.

But that night took on some meaning to forty sons of Uncle Sam
when we realized that we'd just spent another normal night in Nam.

Weeks later, our battalion was in an NDP along Route 13. It was
my job to find and fight the enemy, but enemy activity was light in our
area and contacts were hard to find. The dry season was beginning and
soldiering without getting wet was comforting.

I was sitting outside the battalion command post with my radios that
kept me in constant contact with brigade headquarters. (Battalions worked
for brigades. During one 24-hour period, the 1st of the 18th worked for
all three brigades.) I was listening to the brigade commander talking with
someone on the ground about 10 kilometers north of us. As I said earlier,
before a battalion commander could assume command, the division

commander had him observe the Boss for a week. One of these new battalion commanders, LTC Lewis Menetrey was with me, listening to the fight developing miles to the north. I got a call to bring LTC Menetrey to the NDP of the 2nd Battalion, 28th Infantry as soon as possible.

As we waited for the helicopter, I could tell by the radio traffic that things were not going well. I had no idea how bad it was going to get. The tension and stress in the voices on the radio caused me to realize that serious was a gross under evaluation of the situation. Within a few minutes we were airborne, and shortly had the 2-28's landing zone in sight. As we landed, there was a "slick" (GI slang for a transport helicopter) taking off ahead of us. I was surprised to see a soldier running from the helicopter, not toward the battalion command post, but toward the jungle and the battle. I thought it odd, but odd things happen in combat.

I did not realize it at the time, but I had landed on the periphery of one of the largest ambushes of U.S. forces in the Vietnam War—the battle of Ong Thanh. The brigade commander had asked for LTC Menetrey to come to the 2-28 because their battalion commander had been killed. Two rifle companies of the 2-28 along with the battalion command section, a total of about 175 Big Red One soldiers, had been ambushed by what we learned later was a force of 1,400 Viet Cong. Unknown to me at the time was the fact that a future subordinate, one of the finest officers in the Army, and one of the best friends I have ever had, was fighting for his life a few kilometers away. First Lieutenant Albert Clark Welch, commander or D Company, 2-28 Infantry was in a desperate situation. Although his left bicep muscle had been shot away and he was wounded four more times, Welch continued to fight until he lost consciousness.

I will always believe the soldier I saw running toward the jungle and the "sound of muskets" was Major Donald Holleder, the brigade S-3. Although brave, his attempt to help the 2-28 was futile—he was trying to get to an American battalion that was surrounded by hundreds of Viet Cong. Perhaps because of the excitement, stress and criticality of the situation, he felt compelled to charge into the battle. I think he believed he was the only man who could take over from commanders who had been wounded and killed. He was shot and killed a moment after I saw him running toward the battle. Clark Welch has stated that Holleder was the only one who tried to get to and assist his beleaguered soldiers that day. Of course this is speculation, but perhaps Holleder's courage would not let him conceive that he might be in danger. Did he have the absolute confidence that he could get to the 2-28th and assume command when no one else could? The belief that "Anything you can do, I can do better!" can get one killed. I believe he was suffering from the Ranger Curse and died because of it.

It was days, weeks and years later before I understood the full extent of the action at Ong Thanh. A number of books have been written about this battle, which I know now was an ambush of an Infantry battalion. I did not learn the entire story until Captain Clark Welch became my S-3 when I commanded the Florida Ranger Camp. The 2-28 lost 59 killed (including the battalion commander), and 75 wounded—almost a third of the entire battalion.

An ambush anywhere is deadly for those being ambushed, but in the jungle, it is even more deadly. My experience that day caused me to build my day-to-day life around not being ambushed in matters large or small. As you know, if you are around me in a situation where there is even the slightest possibility of conflict, I will always say, "I don't want to be ambushed!"

That is what happened on October 17, 1967, (ironically, your mother's birthday) to a group of Infantrymen and to Clark Welch, who was awarded the Distinguished Service Cross and to his artillery forward observer, who was awarded the Medal of Honor.

CHAPTER 6

THE RED ELEPHANTS

When someone hisses warm breath onto a shiny object like a chrome car bumper, the resulting vapor causes the reflections to be misty, vague and obscured. After 40 years, many of the events that were a part of my tour in Vietnam have faded like the images reflected in misty chrome. While time fogs the memory, there are certain events that never lose their clarity. One thing that remains stark in my mind, as much as I wish it would fade, is the memory of the Red Elephants.

I am an Infantryman. I have carried the "grunt" stigma with incredible pride all my life. In fact I enjoy the ribbing from officers of other branches and services who constantly opine that only those lacking in social and intellectual skills become Infantrymen. But those of us who wear the crossed rifles know for certain that we are a cut above.

Infantry officers learn from our training, and from senior commanders and mentors, certain time-honored traditions that may or may not be written in field manuals. For example, there are two rules that all Infantry officers know instinctively from the time they first lace up their combat boots: Always accomplish the mission and always take care of the troops. Note that "accomplish the mission" comes first. The Red Elephants episode caused me to rethink which rule should be paramount. In fact, the event caused me to look upon the two rules differently for the rest of my life.

By October of 1967, my crossed rifles had placed me as the operations officer (S-3) of the First Battalion, 18th Infantry of the 1st U.S. Army Infantry Division, "The Big Red One". Only in later years have I truly come to appreciate the importance of such a job. To have been given such a prestigious assignment was an honor in itself. But on top of that, to get to work for the best commander in the Army was an experience I will value forever. He was, all rolled together, teacher, mentor, ass-chewer, and best friend. To me, he was simply "the Boss".

The Boss was also the division commander's fair-haired boy. With that seemingly innocent title came the burden of his battalion always being immediately available for every dangerous and difficult mission that came along. Such was the Boss's reputation that the division commander ordered all incoming battalion commanders to spend time in our battalion headquarters observing how he operated.

In October in our Area of Operations (AO), some 75 miles north of Saigon, it was then the dry season. Of course fighting continued during the rainy season, but the dry season was traditionally the time of heavy fighting, since observation, flight operations, and maneuver on the ground were easier. Our battalion had seen few days without large and small scale fire fights. (A note for anyone who hasn't seen Infantry combat first hand: From the soldier's viewpoint, all fire fights, whether at squad level or at company or battalion level, are big firefights. Therefore, to our troopers, our battalion was in constant close combat with a determined enemy.)

My battalion had been air lifted into the area near Song Be, a truly beautiful part of Vietnam along the Cambodian border. It was, I was told, where the royal and the rich, both French and Vietnamese, vacationed during earlier, peaceful times. Song Be was a quaint old village where the province chief and his staff (including American advisors and some CIA operatives) lived in luxury. (They once gave me permission to use their shower.) Song Be was in the shadow of Nui Ba Ra, a mountain that seemingly sprang straight up from surrounding lush jungle greenery, rice fields, and rubber plantations.

As a sign of the faith the Boss had in me, he left me in near complete control of daily operations. As I found out, total faith in a subordinate can sometimes be dangerous. Such as the time, from a helicopter, I misread the map and placed a "no-fire-line" behind the battalion's position on the ground. A no-fire-line is a control measure that keeps supporting fires from hitting our troops and is placed in front of friendly positions. My mistake left the Boss and our troops vulnerable not only to the enemy, but our own gunships, artillery, and tac-air. In short, I had put him in danger and had taken away his supporting fires.

Over the radio, he simply said, "Dog-face Three, this is Six—You're fired! Meet me at the CP if I get out of this alive".

With the help of his God and my luck, no troops were killed and the no-fire line was removed with a "Flash" message from me. Flash messages are the highest priority in the signal world and are rarely if ever used. It was the only one I ever gave over the radio in my 22 years of service. A few hours later, I went to see the Boss.

He looked up at me and said, "Tough day."

I said, "Yes, sir."

He then asked, "Have you eaten?"

I replied, "I don't think I'm hungry."

Anyway, I had supper and the incident was never mentioned until years later. I never again established a no-fire-line without absolute certainty about my map reading. The Boss's other absolute was that I could not commit the reserve unless he was dead. Thank God I never had to commit the reserve.

Another example of the operational freedom the Boss entrusted to me was the use of his helicopter. The battalion had the use of an OH-13 Flying Bubble helicopter from the division aviation battalion on a daily basis. As the S-3, I could use the helicopter any time I wanted as long as the Boss wasn't using it.

These OH-13s were flown by warrant officers who were nothing but kids. Many were still teenagers when they graduated from flight school. I hated to see them without their helmets, because they looked as if they should still be at home, pumping gas and taking their favorite girls to the movies. Instead, they were combat pilots, and kids or not, they were the best, many of them hot-shots. One of these kids, at the end of the day when he was going back to the aviation battalion, would lift off and fly backwards out of our night defensive position. The troops loved to watch his antics and always gave him an ovation.

One day, our chopper was late. When he arrived, I was about to admonish the pilot when he said, "Major, you won't believe what I just saw!"

I said, "OK, what did you see?"

He said, "A herd of red elephants!"

I answered, "Chief, you spent too much time at the club last night!" (Chief was a common nickname for warrant officer pilots. It was a shortening of the rank of Chief Warrant Officer.)

He insisted, "No kidding, I'm telling you the truth! They are about ten klicks south."

I said, "OK, let's go take a look."

I normally carried a .45 caliber pistol and a CAR-15, a short version of the M-16, which I hated. At this time in Vietnam, there were still a few M-14s that fired a 7.62 NATO round (.30 caliber). When the Army took away the M-14s and issued the lighter M-16s, which had a tendency to jam, the troops practically went into mourning.

I turned to a soldier who was armed with an M-14 and asked, "May I borrow your weapon?"

He said, "Sure, sir, if you will get it back to me."

I said, "Of course", and he threw in a couple of extra magazines.

Before we took off, I told my operations sergeant to check with the Vietnamese province chief to see if there were any wild elephants in the area. The area was filled with incredible wildlife: tigers, monkeys, apes, deer (ranging from moose-size to miniature), and birds that darkened the sky when they took to wing in the afternoon.

I received the answer that there were no wild elephants in the area. The only elephants, said the province chief, belonged to the North Vietnamese Army and the Viet Cong, who used them as pack animals. He said if we came across them, they should be destroyed. He also stated that we could expect any elephants we found to be accompanied by their handlers.

We took off and flew southwest for 15 to 20 minutes. Suddenly, the pilot said, "That's where they were."

The area below was a sea of neck-high grass with islands of palm trees and groves of bamboo. There was a large tree line four of five hundred meters to the west that was the beginning of endless triple-canopy jungle. We circled a few times and landed once where the grass was only knee high. There was no sign of animal or human life. The chief and I exchanged casual banter centered on his lack of visual reconnaissance skill.

His response was an unwavering, "Major, they were here!"

I acknowledged his statement and said, "OK, let's go back."

We lifted off and as we did a slow left turn, I looked over his shoulder, and by God, there they were. I pointed to them and the chief turned harder to the left and began a slow decent. The hairs on the back of my neck stood erect as I remembered the province chief's warning that Vietcong handlers could be expected to accompany the elephants.

The chief and I discussed what I was about to do and he maneuvered the chopper so that I could have a clear shot out of the starboard side of the aircraft. The elephants were red as he had said, no doubt from rolling in the bright red laterite soil of the area. There were five of them. One was very large and had extremely long tusks. I had never been close to an elephant except the ones in the Memphis zoo.

I didn't think much about their appearance at the time, because I had a mission: to kill them. Later the memory of their eyes began to haunt me. There was nothing wild or fierce about their eyes. They were penetrating and knowing.

The chief gently set the chopper down and I turned 45 degrees placing my right foot on the skid. I didn't think much about what I did then. As the chief pulled pitch, I looked back on my act as just another necessity of the war. The Vietnam War was about killing after all, wasn't it? We circled the area and I got my artillery support officer on the radio. I told him I had an enemy location and wanted fire on it. I had seen no handlers, but the province chief said they were there, so I acted accordingly. The artillery officer said there were no 105mm near enough, but the 155mm and 8-inchers were. I gave him the coordinates and cleared the area for incoming. We headed back to Song Be, the chief having proved himself right, and I having done my job—or so I thought. A sad footnote: Several days later, the chopper was again late. When it became obvious that the aircraft would not be arriving, division aviation began a search. I was extremely saddened to learn that my friend the Chief had been shot down and killed.

It wasn't until later, when I saw another herd of elephants that I realized that there were in fact wild elephants in our area. There had been no handlers with the five I had killed. I now knew that they had been wild also. Since that time, I have constantly wished that time would fog the memory of that day, but the reflections remain too vivid.

The down time at the Song Be air strip continued—short relatively safe platoon and company patrols that checked out the rubber trees in the beautiful Terra Rouge area. As I planned daily operations, I found myself keeping the troops out of the dense jungle, where movement was nearly impossible and danger lurked. As I visited the troops I began to realize that the looks that I saw in their eyes were strangely familiar: penetrating and knowing—like the looks in the eyes of the elephants. Again, one of John's poems explains it well:

ON KNOWING by John Gross

Sometimes you could look at one of them
And know he wouldn't make it
Everything about him
His whole being cried out:
"Let me live!"
But you knew
He wouldn't

My mission was clear. It was the mission of all Infantrymen in battle throughout the ages: Close with and kill or capture the enemy. Accomplish the mission. Take care of the troops. But as I looked into the eyes of our soldiers, I knew that I had reversed the two rules. I had been taking care of the troops by not sending them into the heavy jungle. I had put their safety ahead of accomplishing the mission. Was I derelict in my duties?

The Boss had been under unbearable pressure for six months and the strain on him was obvious to me. I don't think it was obvious to others. When I saw him spending extra time with the Catholic chaplain, I knew he was anguishing. He was a devout Catholic and I knew he could not, without the help of the priest, rid himself of the anguish over our troops that had been killed and the ones he knew would be killed. The Boss knew his tour of command was nearing its end. A few more months and the burden of combat would be shifted to another. I knew he was uncomfortable with that thought. Without any arrogance, he knew he could keep his soldiers alive better than a new commander, whose mistakes would cost lives. As I watched his agony, I realized he was a soldier who wanted to do his duty—a soldier who loved his troops but was helpless to stop the killing. It became clear to me that he felt the same way that I did, but could never admit his feelings to anyone. We had reversed the rules. For both of us they now read: Take care of the troops, then do your best to accomplish the mission. This philosophy stayed with me until the end of my combat duty. I would use maneuver, air support, artillery, gun ships—anything that would keep me from sending our troops into direct, deadly combat with the enemy.

The Boss taught me well—let the artillery do the killing. That is why today, when I visit with young officers who have served in combat or soon will, I always tell them they are poor leaders if they ever let their artillery forward observer stray more than an arms length from them. I tell them they should keep their forward observers so close that the FOs would begin to smell like they do.

Was I derelict in my duties? Many other Vietnam combat leaders admit they felt the same way I did. Lives are too valuable to throw into the meat grinder as was done at Gettysburg, the Somme in WW I, the Hurtgen Forrest in WWII, Heartbreak Ridge in Korea, and Hamburger Hill in Vietnam. I remember reading about General Douglas MacArthur's statement to President Roosevelt: "Good commanders do not turn in high casualty rates." To this day, I know the Boss felt the same way I did: Take care of the troops. Accomplish the mission with firepower, not bodies.

CHAPTER 7

THE C-130 PIT STOP

In October, 1967, my battalion had established a night defensive position near the airfield at the village of Song Be, adjacent to the Cambodian border. I was serving as the operations officer (S-3) of the battalion.

Early one afternoon, an Air Force C-130 transport aircraft landed at the airstrip. As it touched down, it blew a tire, not a really big deal, since there were three other main gear tires to support the plane. But taking off with a flat tire presented a problem. The crew had to change the tire.

The aircrew seemed to enjoy the sunny fall-like weather. Shirts off, they horse-played, joked and tossed a football. After ordering a new tire, they continued to enjoy their down time. The new tire was delivered a short time later, but the crew seemed to be in no particular hurry to leave.

I had no authority over the Air Force crew or their schedule, so I paid little attention to their actions. But I knew one thing they didn't. Every afternoon at or just prior to sunset, the Viet Cong would lob mortar shells into our position or onto the airfield. The mortars were not the big stuff like the 82mm or 120mm, but rather the smaller 60mm rounds. As I watched the aircrew enjoying their fun, the thought came to my mind that with that nice big target sitting stationary on the airstrip, the enemy gunners just might up their firepower.

Nothing much was going on in our Tactical Operations Center (TOC), so I ambled over to the airplane.

I watched the crew throw their football for a minute, then I asked the crew chief, "Have you ever been mortared?"

"No, why?" he asked.

"Well, you are about to be," I answered, "and you guys are welcome in my bunker."

No words can describe what happened next. Like a Keystone Cops silent movie, the crew burst into action. Mario Andretti's pit crew would have been impressed at the speed at which the tire was changed. The first propeller began to turn before the flat had been loaded on the airplane, and the C-130 began to roll before the crew chief had put his shirt back on. After the world's shortest take-off run, the C-130 climbed out at a surprisingly steep angle and disappeared into the setting sun.

Until this day, I chuckle when I remember the Air Force pit crew changing their tire. And I always enjoy telling the tale to blue suiters I meet.

CHAPTER 8

FAREWELL TO COMBAT

General James Longstreet reportedly said at the battle of Gettysburg, "Somehow I've never thought about those boys in blue as the enemy." In 2002, Lieutenant Colonel (Retired) Clark Welch had the opportunity to return to Vietnam to help Pulitzer Prize winner David Maraniss do research for his book, *They Marched Into Sunlight, War and Peace in Vietnam and America,* which was in great part about the battle of Ong Thanh. During that trip, Welch met the Viet Cong commander he had fought on 17 October, 1967. They walked hand in hand about the battlefield, exchanging memories of the battle. They became good friends. Likewise, most Infantrymen in Vietnam harbored no malice toward the enemy we were fighting. In fact, many soldiers even admired the tenacity, skill and courage of the Viet Cong and the North Vietnamese. Many Infantrymen expressed a certain comradeship with the enemy soldiers who were trying to kill them. After all, rain fell equally on both sides, and mosquitoes and leaches drew blood from the VC as well as GIs. Of course there were exceptions to this, especially when the enemy had killed a trooper's best friend or family member. Then, hatred and rage often followed. I never harbored hatred or anger toward the enemy. I killed them, like I killed the red elephants, simply because it was my job. And working for the Boss, I became very good at it. I got no adrenalin rush or emotional stimulation from killing. My keenest emotion was to feel sorry for the poor bastard lying there, blown to bits. I often imagined how an enemy soldier must have felt. I could almost feel the fear and horror he must have had as he charged forward, knowing he was about to die. I respect any Infantryman, regardless of his nationality, who pays the ultimate price for doing his job.

During World War II, most communications took place over field telephone lines. Each headquarters switchboard had a distinctive name. In the First Infantry Division, all of these switchboard names began with the letter "D". For example, the division switchboard was named "Danger". During the Vietnam War, the division continued the "D" tradition, this time for radio call signs. When the Boss took command of our battalion, the 1-18's call sign was "Duchess", hardly a name for a combat battalion. The Boss quickly changed our name to "Dogface", after a line in an old soldiers' song, "I don't want to be a sailor or a fancy-pants Marine, I'd rather be the dogface soldier that I am". The commander always had the call sign of "Six", the executive officer was "Five", and the staff officers were one through four. The S-1, or personnel officer was "Dogface 1", the intelligence officer was "Dogface 2", the operations officer—my job—was "Dogface 3", and the logistics officer was "Dogface 4". To this day, I refer to the Boss as "Dogface 6".

I was extremely sad when it was time for the Boss to say goodbye to his beloved "Dogface" battalion. The normal length of a battalion command tour in Vietnam was six months. Incredibly, the Boss had been in command of the 1-18 for ten months. As I have stated, all incoming battalion commanders in the division had to spend a week with our battalion. Lieutenant Colonel George Tronsrue had been with us for a few weeks, observing our operations, and when the Boss departed, he became our new commander.

One requirement a professional officer is that when a change of command takes place, he must immediately transfer all his loyalty and commitment to the new commander. Throughout my career, I automatically did this, since it cleared the air and gave the new commander the benefit of the doubt as he began to earn respect on his own. Despite my devotion to Boss, I hope I did this for George Tronsrue. I did my best to keep him from making any mistakes that would cost any trooper his life as he learned how to be a combat commander. He turned out to be a fine leader.

Thankfully, during this time our battalion had a break from battle. There was no sign of the enemy anywhere. In retrospect, the VC were probably lying low getting ready for January's Tet Offensive. We had a

Christmas visit from Bob Hope and I went on R&R to Hawaii to meet your mother. When I arrived in jungle fatigues, she placed a garland of flowers around my neck with a kiss and said, "Your first lei of the day!" It was a wonderful way to end the year of 1967.

As the new year dawned, we all hoped 1968 would see then end of the war. We listened to radio broadcasts about U.S. efforts to negotiate peace with the North Vietnamese. As odd as it seems now, I had the feeling at that time that the war was over. No unit in our entire area could find any trace of the enemy. Though our task was to "close with and kill or capture the enemy", the lack of contact didn't at all make me feel that we weren't doing our jobs. In fact, the absence of combat was wonderful. Like the Boss, LTC Tronsrue allowed me to run the combat operations of the battalion without much supervision.

In mid-January, Dogface moved to an area west of Lai Khe. The dry season and the lack of combat made for good duty. Lai Khe offered shade from rubber trees and clear landing zones for resupply helicopters. It is still hard to believe that everything a four-hundred-man battalion in the field needed could be brought in by helicopter. We wanted for nothing.

At Lai Khe, my daily routine was to do an aerial reconnaissance in our H-13 helicopter. I would fly over an area to help me plan the next day's patrols. Patrols were normally company size—100 or more Infantrymen with an artillery forward observer. Since we had had no significant contact for months, I had reduced the size of most patrols near our night defensive position (NDP) to that of a platoon—20 to 40 troopers.

One morning, when my chopper arrived, I selected an area west of Lai Khe known as the Trapezoid, which was just north of the famous Iron Triangle. This area had been very dangerous over the years and the engineers had cleared hundreds of square kilometers with their Rome plows. The remaining area was forested by triple-canopy jungle, meaning that there were enormous trees, with smaller trees growing beneath, and shrubbery near the ground. In triple canopy, sunlight seldom touched the ground. It was the worst kind of terrain for jungle fighting, since most of our supporting fires could not penetrate the thick vegetation. In triple canopy, combat was often Infantryman against Infantryman. As a result, I would not commit our soldiers into this type of jungle without being ordered to do so.

As my pilot and I flew along, I noted obstacles on the map. Several streams crossed the area. The clear water made the depth deceptive. What appeared to be shallow water could be six to eight feet deep, a major obstacle to Infantrymen. As we continued west, we flew over ever-thickening jungle, and soon, we were over the triple canopy. As we flew over the jungle, which seemed endless, all we could see were tree tops. Often helicopter-bound senior commanders could not understand why soldiers on the ground were moving so slowly. Unless a commander walked the terrain, he could not conceive of the difficulty involved in walking from Point A to Point B—and many senior commanders did not. When the Boss had been in command, he had often walked with company-sized patrols. No senior commander could critique his unit's movement without incurring his wrath—and his reputation and credibility was such that few senior commanders dared challenge him. In fact, in my years working for the Boss in Vietnam, Fort Riley, and Germany, I never heard of a senior officer attempting to admonish him. Criticism by anyone of equal rank was unheard of and was sure to be career threatening. Throughout the years I have attempted to emulate him, but I know I have failed.

While conducting my aerial reconnaissance, I had a rule that I almost never allowed my pilot to violate. I say almost, since the one time I allowed it, I paid dearly. I told my pilots to never fly over the same spot twice. If a pilot violated this rule, he would be on the receiving end of a severe ass-chewing. Fortunately, my warrant officer pilots were such quick learners that I didn't have to do much admonishing.

When we lifted off that morning, little did I know that I would violate my own rule and that this would be my last day as Dogface 3. As we were flying less than a hundred feet above the tallest trees, I was trying to find holes in the vegetation so I could see signs of Viet Cong activity. Though one hole in the jungle, I could see a trail with deep ruts. I had never seen anything like this before. To confirm what I had seen, I told my pilot to violate my rule and fly over the hole a second time. As he slowly turned and hovered over the spot, I could see more ruts and a donut-shaped machine gun position. After digging a circular trench, the gunner could place the gun on the solid center and run around the trench, giving him a 360-degree field of fire. I saw no enemy soldiers, but looking south along the ruts, I could see boxes stacked neatly along both sides of the trail. In all my time as Dogface 3, I had never seen such a sight. The pilot had slowed the chopper and we hovered so low that the rotor wash was moving the tree tops, allowing me to get a better view of the gun positions and boxes.

As I concentrated on the sights below, all of a sudden gunfire erupted around us. We had both taken ground fire before, so there was no discussion about what to do. As bullets cracked and thudded into the small helicopter, we tried to get the hell away from there. Suddenly, my right leg and thigh became hot and stiff at the same time. I had been hit by bullets and shrapnel that had come up through the bottom of the fuselage and trough my seat. The pilot said he had not been hit but the chopper had been shot up pretty badly. There was no place to land except the NDP, which was a few kilometers away. The only thing I remember about the short flight back to the NDP was the aviation gasoline spewing from the exterior fuel tank. Just like Forest Gump in the movie, I had been "shot in the buttocks". When we landed I was hauled out of the chopper and taken to the medics. I did not have a chance to apologize or thank the pilot, who did a magnificent job of flying a shot-up helicopter to safety. I never saw him again. I hope his name is not on the wall.

The only words I spoke to George Tronsrue were perhaps the most important I ever uttered. I said, "Don't go in there. It is an ambush!"

Remembering the carnage at the Battle of Ong Thanh the previous October, and following my commitment to never place our troops in a position where they had to go head-to-head with the VC in a pitched battle, I hoped the battalion commander would follow my advice. Years later, when we discussed what had happened, he said he had put mortars and artillery into that position, but no troops. I feel I saved a lot of lives with those eight words. Thank God Tronsrue followed my advice. A lot of men who served in the Dogface battalion are alive today because Tronsrue used artillery and not troops with rifles.

But there is another side to this story. If Tronsrue had committed our battalion into that area, he would have had to fight his way in and a much larger force than Dogface would have been required. Once the shooting started, the Big Red One would accept nothing but victory. More and more units would have been piled on until the battle was decided in our favor. While we would have lost many troops, this would have become the first battle of the Tet Offensive. By surprising a major enemy force that had the mission of taking Saigon, Dogface could have prevented much of the combat in and around Saigon on 31 January. If that had been the case, one might speculate that the war could have ended in a much different manner than it did.

I consider my "shoot down" and George's decision not to attack as a pivotal event in the war. Tet was the event that began to turn the majority of American people against the war. A clear win before Tet might have kept the press from claiming that U.S. forces were surprised, and the Tet Offensive might not have been depicted as a strategic defeat for the U.S. The whole outcome of the war might have been different. There is a saying that perception is reality. This is my perception of events that historians will argue about for years to come. But remember, I have an advantage the historians do not have—I was there!

I was evacuated by a "Dustoff" (medical evacuation helicopter) to the MASH (Mobile Army Surgical Hospital) in Le Kei and then moved to the hospital at Long Binh. The care was wonderful and I was able to move around on crutches within a few days. I checked myself out with the help of a young nurse, whose future husband was an armored officer who, as I recall, was serving with the First Squadron of the 4th Cavalry. Part of our agreement for her helping me get "checked out" was that I would "look after him". In this I failed because he was killed in the first few days of Tet.

I spent the remainder of my tour in the G-3 (operations) section at division. I was involved in no more combat, but I watched many battles from the air. On one occasion during Tet, as I flew with General Talbott, I watched as a mechanized cavalry unit trapped a four-hundred man Viet Cong battalion in a ravine. They saturated the gully with bombs and napalm from tactical air and annihilated the enemy. The mech unit suffered few if any casualties. That was the appropriate use of fire power. While serving in the G-3 section, I learned that my replacement as Dogface 3 had been killed. He, like I, was hit by ground fire while doing aerial reconnaissance.

CHAPTER 9

FORT LEAVENWORTH

How is an infantry soldier supposed to feel when he is leaving a combat zone that has been his home for a year? For me, leaving my unit and the soldiers I loved and coming home to family and friends spanned the entire spectrum of human emotion—happiness and elation on one end, and anger, frustration and deep sadness on the other. It is easy to understand the reason for happiness and elation, but I must admit I was more saddened than elated by my departure. Total immersion in daily life-and-death situations coupled with the realization that there was no favorable outcome in sight for our army, viscerally ripped into my soul. I came home with the feeling that there was no winning, no losing, just more and more death and destruction. I was sad to leave the unit, but I was not so remorseful I that I would have voluntarily extended or volunteered for another tour, though some of my fellow Infantrymen did. Often, such extensions and multiple tours carried the death penalty. One of the operations NCOs who worked with me had extended his tour by six months. With the extension had come a period of leave back home in the States. He had just returned and was standing inside a bunker when a 122 millimeter rocket hit the entrance and killed him. Such rare incidents were widely discussed by the troops. In fact, multiple-tour soldiers were perceived to carry a "hex". Some soldiers actually refused to serve near them. Such are the rumors and suspicions that are carried by combat soldiers.

Instant transition from combat to peaceful life in the U.S. to me was like trying to shift a vehicle traveling at high speed into low gear without a clutch. I had come from the high-tension atmosphere of combat to the academic world. I had orders to attend the Command and General Staff College at Fort Leavenworth, Kansas. Nothing seemed real. I got too much rest, too much sleep, and for the first time in a year, I had no stress. Stress had become my closest companion. Even the loving warmth of my family could not alleviate the feeling that without stress, life was not worth living. If I could have felt stress from my academic endeavors, I perhaps could have excelled in my studies, but Leavenworth did not challenge me. Four years later, when I was stationed in Saudi Arabia, I again faced that same demon—the lack of stress and challenge. It seemed that I could not survive without something to constantly stimulate the flow of adrenalin.

Leavenworth was not a total waste. It was there that your mother gave me the wonderful task of helping to create you. My experience in the Vietnam War had convinced me that a family with only one child was a potential catastrophe. Losing a child is devastating to any family. You saw that firsthand with our loss of Carlton (Carlton Tucker died of a heart attack when he was only 38 years old). But losing an only child must double the pain. Therefore, we were determined after ten years to try again. We wanted a daughter. So out came the thermometers, charts, books and rules for abstention. The pain of wanting sex and not being able to have it until the proper time and temperature was excruciating. It was difficult for me to understand, but your mother did. We agreed we wanted a girl and that required special timing in her cycle. The rule for me was that there could be no waste of any sperm through any self-gratification. The motto was "suffer through it." You were the most beautiful baby ever born. When you arrived, I realized that your mother must have known what she was doing.

Near the end of the school year at Ft. Leavenworth, the officer assignment team from the Army's Chief of Personnel came to farm us graduates out around the world. We had been schooled in tactics, the application of fire power, and how to work as staff officers at the general officer level. Most of the staff instruction was alien to me. I could not think much beyond battalion level, and to me, the idea of combat on the plains of Europe, which most of our tactical schooling was based on, was far-fetched. To me, what we studied at Leavenworth was, as British

General Frederick Browning, deputy commander of the First Allied Airborne Army in WWII said, "a bridge too far."

The career briefing officer told me I had an excellent record. I had received two below the zone promotions meaning that I was in the top ten percent of my peers. My assignment officer told me that it was time for me to go to the Pentagon. I knew better. I realized that I was a terrible staff officer and I fully recognized my limitations. A few days after I had been offered what other officers dreamed of, serving at the Pentagon, I made one of the best decisions of my career. The commanding general at Ft. Leavenworth was Lieutenant General John Hay, who had commanded the First Infantry Division in Vietnam. He was now a lieutenant general (three stars). He and Dick Cavazos, my boss in Vietnam, were close and I knew the general well. I asked his secretary to arrange an appointment with him. He and I had seen each other at social gatherings, where he always enjoyed the company of your mother. Loraine was not impressed with rank. She treated him the same way she treated everyone else, with southern charm, warmth, and feminine guile, which he seemed to bask in. She would tell me in front of the general that he was the handsomest general she had ever met.

During my appointment with General Hay, we exchanged pleasantries, then I asked him for a huge favor. I said, "Sir, I don't want to go to Washington. I want to go to Fort Benning." He explained to me something that I had always known: "If you don't serve your time in the Pentagon, then promotions will be hard to get." I explained that promotions weren't the reason for my being an Infantrymen. I told him I served for the troops. I read later that General Eisenhower once told Army chief of staff General George C. Marshall nearly the same thing, that serving and doing the job was what was important, not promotions.

General Hay reached over to his intercom and said, "Get me Buck Newman." Buck had been a brigade commander for General Hay and was now the head of officer assignments at Infantry Branch. I had worked for Buck on numerous occasions while I was "Dogface 3". I hoped he remembered me. General Hay said, "Buck, you remember Tucker, he was Cavazos's S-3. He wants to go to Ft. Benning." Then they talked awhile and he hung up and said, "You will be assigned to Ft. Benning. Good luck." That's all there was to it. The old saying "It's who you know not what you know," came to mind. That phone call changed my life and touched many others as well.

CHAPTER 10

TO FORT BENNING
AND ON TO FLORIDA

For an Infantryman, going back to Fort Benning is like going home. As a matter of fact, many Infantry officers facetiously call Fort Benning Fort Beginning, since we all started there. We went to the Officers' Basic Course, and the Airborne and Ranger courses. As captains, we returned for the 10-month Infantry Officers' Advanced Course. Some then attended the Nuclear, Chemical, and Biological Targeting course. Many of those of us on parachute status attended Jumpmaster School at Benning.

Many of the greats were stationed at Benning. Omar Bradley served as the commandant of the Infantry School prior to World War II. George Patton commanded the Second Armored Division there.

Being an Infantryman carries some negative connotations. Many officers of other branches consider the Infantrymen to be knuckle-dragging Neanderthals. A tongue-in-cheek motto of the artillery is, "We lend dignity to what otherwise would be a vulgar brawl". But deep down, everyone in the Army knows the Infantry to be the most revered branch. The Infantry and combat medics are the only branches that award special badges for service in combat. The Combat Infantryman's Badge (CIB) was established to recognize the fact that the majority of combat casualties in WWII were in the Infantry, and those who survived the rigors of Infantry combat deserved special recognition. It is hard for the Infantryman not to feel superior. God help me, I have always felt superior to those who served in other branches.

When I reported in to Fort Benning, I was surprised to learn that I was to command one of the outlying phases of Ranger School. Both the mountain and Florida Ranger Camps, located in north Georgia and Eglin Air Force Base, Florida, respectively, were part of the Ranger Department of the U.S. Army Infantry School. Although assigned to Benning, we would live and I would command in Florida.

I was required by protocol to stop by the Ranger Department headquarters before going on to Florida. I looked forward to reporting to the department director because Colonel Y.Y. Phillips and I had attended Ranger school together when he was a captain and I was a second lieutenant. When I knocked on his door and reported to him, he sat with his feet on his desk, smoking a big cigar, and reading the Wall Street Journal. It was not like a subordinate reporting to a senior officer, it was more like two old friends getting together after a long time apart. He dropped the paper, took his feet off his desk and asked if Lorraine was okay. He was a warm and gentle man for whom I have always had the utmost respect. After we exchanged a few more pleasantries, he said, "Tucker, don't ever let me be surprised." That was all the guidance I received for what would be the most rewarding and in some respects the craziest and most dangerous job I had in my Infantry Career.

The Florida Ranger Camp was located at Auxiliary Field 7, some 25 miles north of Fort Walton Beach, in the pine forests of the Eglin Air Force Base reservation. Our new home (your first home) was in a World War II wooden barracks building. Your mom was carrying you at the time and enjoying every minute of it, because she could eat all she wanted and blame it on the need to properly nourish you. Lorraine quickly turned the old barracks into a warm and inviting home. She loved to give parties and, for the first time in our career, had plenty of room for entertaining.

Shortly after I arrived, I was notified that Air Force Colonel Harry C. (Heinie) Aderholt, commander of the Special Operations Wing stationed at Hurlburt Field was coming to see me. The Special Operations Wing was the outfit that supported our Special Forces with both close air support and logistics. Our Rangers loved the Special Ops wing because they flew low and slow enough so they could see both us and the enemy—and they knew the difference. They flew special propeller-driven aircraft, A-1 Skyraiders,

OV-10 Broncos, U-10 Couriers, O-1 Bird Dogs, C-123 Providers, and several versions of the C-130 Hercules. They loved having the Rangers nearby to train with and they gave us any and all support we asked for. Heinie Aderhold was then and until this day one of the finest officers I have ever known, and I believe history will treat him extremely well. He understood the necessity of close and accurate fire support from aircraft. Many in the Air Force at that time did not fully grasp the importance of close air support. They were focused on air superiority.

I was still a major when I assumed command of the Ranger camp. Heinie honored me by coming to Field 7 to promote me to lieutenant colonel. Heinie had a unique career, during which he received three Article 15s by a four-star general. On the day that general retired, Heinie was promoted to brigadier general. I was at Heinie's first retirement party at Hurlburt, where, in his retirement speech, he called the four-star a son-of-a-bitch. Some of the senior officers were holding napkins over their faces or pretending to pick up something off of the floor so they would not be photographed laughing.

At Heinie's retirement, a group of Rangers and Air Force Combat Controllers jumped in to the Hurlburt officers' club to add a touch of excitement to the festivities. Unfortunately for me, the jump was a little too exciting. When I exited the aircraft, it was immediately obvious to me that I would not make land. The club was on the shores of Santa Rosa Sound, and I knew I was headed for the water. When I splashed into the sound, I began to search for my life vest to give me buoyancy, but my gear had shifted and I couldn't reach it. Swimming was impossible with all the gear I had on and the parachute began to drag me down. I somehow got to the surface for a breath a couple of times, but I knew I would not be able to surface a third time. I accepted the fact that I was going to drown. Then a pair of strong fisherman's hands grabbed me and lifted me up so I could get air. He pulled me to shallow water and said, "So long". I guess I thanked him. He had just saved an Infantryman from an inglorious death by drowning. I'm not sure Heinie's or anyone else ever knew about this episode. Even after being shot down and wounded in Vietnam, this was the closest I ever felt to death.

I soon found out that the Florida Ranger Camp was like no other command in the Army. It was tremendously rewarding duty since we were training young leaders how to keep their soldiers alive in Vietnam. The training was realistic and challenging, but it was also hazardous. The abnormal, the unusual, and the dangerous were routine. An uncontrolled forest fire could easily be started by a smoke grenade. Ranger instructors who were exhausted from walking great distances with Ranger students could get themselves killed or injured driving or riding motorcycles 25 miles on lonely roads to their homes. One day during a parachute jump a gust of wind carried a Ranger student so fast that when he hit the ground, and failed to do a proper parachute landing fall, his head was crushed and he was killed. On another day, a driver flipped a military vehicle and died because he could not remove watery sand from his mouth and nose. On still another day, an Air Force load master died when he fell from the door of a C-123 without a parachute. Also, I was acutely aware that before I became commander, Ranger students had drowned, been snake bitten, killed by lightning, and died of hypothermia. No matter how safety conscious we all were, the weather and the difficulty of the training challenged us on a daily basis. Florida Ranger Camp commanders always have to ask themselves on a continuous basis, "What are the three worst things that can happen today?" Then they have to plan to keep any of them from happening.

The curriculum during 1969-1971 was different from what Ranger students undergo today, but many aspects of Ranger school have never changed and never will. The U.S. Army Ranger School in 1969-1971 was (and still is) about 9 weeks long and, with the possible exception of Navy SEAL training, was and still is the toughest training in our military. It consisted of three phases. The first three-weeks was known as the Benning Phase. It consisted of physical training, obstacle courses, hand-to-hand combat, bayonet drill, road marches, demolitions, artillery fire adjustment, survival, and patrolling training.

The second three-week phase was the Mountain Phase, conducted at the Mountain Ranger Camp near Dalhonega, Georgia (I was an instructor in the mountains as a first lieutenant. Remember I was stationed there when Carlton was born.) In the mountain phase, Ranger students learned mountaineering, including knot-tying, free and party climbing, rappelling, and rope bridging. The bulk of the mountain phase training consisted of brutal simulated combat operations in the Blue Ridge Mountains.

Following the mountain phase, the Ranger students were trucked back to Fort Benning, where they prepared for a parachute insertion into the Florida Phase. (Captain Clark Welch, my operations officer or S-3, originated the parachute insertion of Ranger students into Florida. He did a staff study comparing the cost of contracting civilian busses for the trip to Florida to jumping the students in. He found that the parachute jump could be paid for by the Air Force by classifying the jump as "Joint Army/ Air Force training (JAAT)", thereby saving the Army a ton of money. The parachute insertion of Ranger students into Florida, known as Operation Stiletto, is still ongoing today, 40 years after Captain Welch originated it. When the students landed in Florida, they in-processed, then underwent a week of technique training. In Florida, we taught water and swamp operations. The technique training consisted of river crossing using the one-rope bridge, constructing poncho rafts, small boat operations, snake safety, counter-ambush drill, jungle quick-kill live fire, night live fire ambush, helicopter rappelling, and visual tracking.

During technique training, instructors worked from 6 a.m. until sometimes 11:30 p.m. for a week straight. Then the students began a twelve-day continuous patrolling operation. During this Field Training Exercise (FTX), the students walked 18-20 hours per day. No sleep was planned and they were issued only one C-ration meal per day. The idea was to make the students so tired and hungry that they thought they could not take another step. Then they would be given another mission, and the training went on and on.

There were three companies or "committees" of instructors—A, B, and C. During the FTX, instructors' duties were split. One committee provided the command and control, supply and administration, while the other two committees provided "walkers". The committees rotated duties, each responsible for planning and controlling four days of the FTX. The walkers, one officer and one NCO, accompanied each platoon of about 40 ranger students. Each walker evaluated four students during a 24-hour period. During each 24-hour period, the student platoon would routinely walk 8-10 kilometers in tactical formation trough the swamps and woods. The captain walker graded the student platoon leaders and the NCO walker graded the student platoon sergeants. The four grades consisted of, first, planning and giving the operation order for the mission; second, navigating to the objective; third, actions at the objective; and fourth, navigating to the link-up site. Ranger students had to pass 50% of their graded patrols to be awarded the Ranger Tab.

At the link-up site, the walkers would critique the platoon and a fresh pair of instructors would relieve them. Outgoing walkers would go back to camp, report their grades, go home, write up their observation reports (grades), get a night's sleep, and go back and do the whole thing over again.

During the FTX, the Ranger students had to plan and execute a parachute jump, a river crossing, a rubber boat movement down a river, an airmobile operation, an amphibious operation, and miles and miles of just plain walking. Instructors changed every 24 hours—the Ranger students continued on without a break throughout the twelve-day exercise.

An enormous amount of planning and preparation took place during the four-day breaks between classes. In 1969, the camp was at Field 7, where, except for the headquarters building, there was no air conditioning anywhere in the camp. Committee rooms were in tin shacks or were located in WWII-era wooden barracks buildings. During the summer, instructors could often be seen walking around the camp barefooted, without shirts, wearing only jungle fatigue pants and the ever-present Ranger patrol cap. If it got too hot during the day, they would pile into a jeep and drive about a mile north to a dammed-up swimming hole in a stream. They would splash about for a few minutes, then go back to work soaking wet.

At the Ranger camp, we had no privates to do the dirty work. The only personnel assigned to the camp were a lieutenant colonel commander, a major who was the executive officer, a sergeant major, and a bunch of captains and senior sergeants. When work had to be done, we all pitched in together and did it. Rank did not matter. For example, if we were building a mock Vietnamese village for training purposes, officers and NCOs worked side by side digging trenches, filling sand bags, thatching roofs, and hammering and nailing.

We were young, we were in fantastic physical shape, and we believed in what we were doing. We had a tremendous sense of accomplishment as we passed our combat experience to young lieutenants and sergeants. Sometimes we would get letters from Vietnam saying something like, "If you had not taught me what you did in Ranger School, I would have been killed today."

There were no Ranger battalions in those days. The Ranger Department of the U.S. Army Infantry School was the only assignment in the Army where a soldier could truthfully say he was an Airborne Ranger!

I remember one captain saying, "You know, I believe I'd be doing this even if the Army didn't pay me." I think we all felt that way.

When I arrived to command the Florida Ranger Camp, I found the conditions at Auxiliary Field 7 to be abysmal. The camp's temporary

World War II barracks and support buildings were in terrible shape. They apparently had had no maintenance since they were built. There was no air conditioning in any building except the headquarters. The mess hall was in a manufactured metal building with a cement floor. In all the buildings, windows, plumbing, and roofs badly needed repair, and all buildings needed paint. The condition of the camp seemingly didn't bother any of the instructors, who cheerfully went about their duties. The camp was 25 miles from Eglin main base, a long drive after walking for 24 hours grading Ranger students.

Soon after I became commander, I received word that the camp was to move approximately ten miles to Auxiliary Field 6, which was the home of a minimum-security federal prison. This was good news, for the facilities at Field 6, while old, had been maintained by the Federal Bureau of Prisons in a much better condition than those at Field 7. In addition, the airfield was long enough to land C-119, C-123, and C-130 aircraft, which we used for parachute jumps. Also, there were several sets of family quarters at Field 6. For the first time, the commander and some key staff personnel would not have to drive over 25 miles to and from work every day and would be available at the camp full time in case of emergencies. The Ranger Camp is still located at Field 6. Today it is known as Camp Rudder, named after the commander of the Second Ranger Battalion of World War II fame, who, with his Rangers, assaulted the cliffs at Point Du Hoc during the Normandy Invasion. In 1969-1971, the camp was simply called the Florida Ranger Camp. Today, Camp Rudder is home to the Sixth Ranger Training Battalion.

The move to Field 6 went smoothly, mainly due to the efforts of my executive officer, Major Bob Frix. Bob was one of the finest officers I ever served with. He ended his extraordinary career as a major general. Since no low-ranking enlisted soldiers were assigned to the camp, my captains and senior NCOs pitched in to load and unload trucks, carry furniture, and reposition vehicles, boats, and supplies. Finally, everything had been moved except the alligators. Big John and One Eye were our two camp mascots at that time. Big John was a 14 footer who had been at the camp since it was formed in the 1950s. One Eye was a smaller female that had lost an eye. Moving One Eye was not much trouble. We taped her mouth shut and immobilized her legs and lifted her onto a deuce-and-a-half truck. Big John was another story. Not only was his gaping mouth a potential danger, but a slap with his massive tail could have broken a leg.

After much head-scratching and hemming and hawing by my instructors, I believe it was Sergeant First Class Joe Leblanc who suggested we secure him to a large 4" X 8" board we had available. Some brave soul lassoed Big John's mouth, taped it shut, and tied it to the board. Then we got a rope around his tail and tied his huge body to the board at several places. Then it took almost every man in the camp to lift him onto a truck. We found that securing him to the board was much easier than releasing him at Field 6. When his tail was untied, everyone jumped back as his tail swept a wide swath. Free at last, he submerged himself in his new pond and didn't come out for days. Big John lived at Field 6 until he died in 2003, at which time he was estimated to be over 100 years old. He is buried next to one of the ponds where he lived for 50 years.

I have never had reservations about calling a general officer or a politician if I needed a favor. I have learned since that time that asking for help from generals or politicians is a rare thing for officers to do. Generals have never intimidated me. I have known many general officers and many have helped me at various times in my career. I have not known many politicians but Lorraine's family had connections to Senator John Stennis. As an Infantryman, I have always used all the supporting fires available to me. I have always looked at generals and politicians as supporting artillery to help me accomplish my mission.

Although Field 6 was in much better shape than Field 7, it still needed work, and there was no funding available to improve the camp. That's where Congressman Bob Sikes came in. Bob Sikes, affectionately known as the "He Coon", represented Florida's first congressional district and was the chairman of the House Military Construction Subcommittee. I had met the congressman at several cocktail parties and he often asked me about the Rangers. Sikes was involved in many things, but his main goal was to protect and grow the military establishment in Northwest Florida. He loved the Rangers, because, he said, "If you fly over a piece of land, you fly over it. If you walk on it you own it." He was constantly worried that civilian developers would chip away at the Eglin Air Force Base reservation. He encouraged the Rangers to walk over every inch of woodland and swamp of Eglin AFB. Boots on the ground, he felt, would help protect Eglin from civilian encroachment.

At one party, Sikes asked about the move from Field 7 to Field 6. I told him all was going well, but I could use some funding to make life at the camp more pleasant. It was for me an offhand response with no request attached. I forgot all about our conversation until I got a call from his Washington office a few weeks later telling me that someone would be coming by to see me. Later, a young man in a well-tailored suit showed up and introduced himself as one of Congressman Sikes' aides. I walked him around the area and explained the potential the little camp had, and pointed out areas that needed improvement. I mentioned that most of my officers and NCOs had to drive a 50-mile round trip to simply come to work. I pointed out that some additional family quarters would make life easier for our instructors. After he left, I soon forgot about his visit.

Several weeks later, I received a call from Major General Orwin Talbott, the commanding general of Fort Benning. The Florida Ranger Camp was part of the Infantry School, which he commanded.

I answered the phone by saying, "Good morning, Sir."

I had worked for General Talbott in Vietnam when he was the assistant division commander of the Big Red One. During the Tet Offensive, Talbot was the senior general present in the division. I had just returned from the hospital after being shot down and he commandeered me to be his flying aide during the Tet battles.

He said, "Tucker, what in the hell is going on down there?"

Talbott was the least profane man I have ever known. For him to use the word "hell" was highly unusual.

I answered, "Sir, I don't know what you are talking about."

"I can't get enough funding at Fort Benning to buy toilet paper, and you just got a million dollars for construction at the Florida Ranger Camp!"

I explained what had happened when Sikes' aide had visited. Thank goodness General Talbot didn't get into "Why didn't you tell me about his visit when it happened?" I guess I should have told someone, but, as I said, I soon forgot about the visit and I had Rangers to train.

The modern Rangers who enjoy the relatively modern facilities at Camp Rudder, as Field 6 is now known, can thank Congressman Sikes. He has always been one of my heroes. I know for sure that the continued presence of the Rangers at Eglin is a direct result of his influence. His belief that boots on the ground would keep the developers away from the Eglin reservation must have had merit. As far as I know, not a single inch of military land has been lost. In fact, the forthcoming basing of the 7th Special Forces Group at Eglin is largely due to Congressman Sikes' foresight.

CHAPTER 11

BACK TO THE BIG RED ONE

I guess you might wonder why, after two years of rigorous Ranger command, your dad might want to go straight to another command assignment. I believe that a dedicated Infantry officer should either be serving in combat, in school, or commanding Infantry soldiers who are training for combat. I also believe the Army makes a mistake in attempting to prepare all officers to be the chief of staff of the Army. I believe there are enough professional staff officers to fill other positions, but there are relatively few who have "fire in the belly" and are natural commanders. I believe these officers should be identified early in their careers and groomed for command at each level. Hugh Shelton and Dick Cavazos are examples of outstanding officers who commanded at every level from captain to four-star general. I often thought that the Army was pushed and pulled along by 10 percent of the officer corps, and the others were just along for the ride. In short, if I could have commanded Infantry soldiers my whole career, I would have done so.

Perhaps the most challenging command position in the Army is the Infantry battalion. This is the highest position where the commander is actually in daily contact with the soldiers. An Infantry battalion can have as many as a thousand troops and hundreds of vehicles and large pieces of equipment. I never got to command in combat, but I feel that being Dick Cavazos' operations officer in Vietnam was very close.

Few, if any, officers get the opportunity to serve with a battalion in combat, then return to command that same unit stateside during peacetime. And fewer still get to serve a second time for a commander like Dick Cavazos. I had that opportunity.

When the First Division stood down in Vietnam, it moved to Fort Riley, Kansas. As much as I loved the Florida Ranger Camp command, when I was offered the chance to go to Fort Riley and take command of the First Battalion, 18th Infantry, I was ecstatic. Not only was I thrilled to return to the 1-18, Dick Cavazos was to be my brigade commander.

To your Mom and Carlton, it was just one more move (The move to Ft. Riley was our fifteenth. Our final move to Fort Walton Beach was number 20.) I never heard either one of them complain, except to say they would miss their friends. I believe they never complained because they were looking forward to meeting new friends at the new post. The nomadic Army life helped your brother develop an outgoing personality and the courage to travel the world in his sailing career. He never met a stranger. I believe most military brats share the same experiences.

Transitioning from the Florida Ranger Camp, which was a training organization, to a TO&E (Table of Organization and Equipment) battalion which had to be ready to go to combat on a moment's notice, was a tremendous leap. There is no way one commander can control 1000 soldiers without a dynamic staff and company commanders who are capable of functioning in a demanding, high-pressure atmosphere. I was once again lucky to have outstanding subordinates who gave me all I asked for and more.

I was doubly lucky since I did not have to learn the ways of my brigade commander. I hit the ground running with the same confidence I had working for him in Vietnam. He simply expected me to always exceed his expectations. I hope I always did.

The training mission was severe. We worked 70 hours a week doing individual and unit training, preparing for IG and maintenance inspections, and pulling a dizzying variety of details and taskings. Every morning began with the Army's "Daily Dozen" exercises and a run of two to four miles in length. On top of that, we routinely went to the field for training exercises that lasted five to ten days at a time without returning to our barracks. In addition we were under the gun to prove our combat readiness by constantly passing spot checks and surprise inspections of every sort.

In 1972 my battalion was part of a larger force that deployed on an exercise known as REFORGER, an acronym for Return of Forces to Germany. REFORGER was primarily a logistical exercise designed to test all the methods of transporting troops and their equipment from a stateside Army post to Germany. This was during the cold war when we feared the possibility that the Russians might attack Western Europe. We had to know how to reinforce Europe as quickly as possible and the only way to do this was to practice. We railed equipment and vehicles to U.S. ports and loaded them on ships which then sailed to European ports. At the same time, we flew our soldiers in on civilian contract airliners and military airlift. Once we arrived and assembled the battalion, we participated in war games that approximated what we would have to do if the Russians poured into West Germany. REFORGER was an extremely demanding mission that required months of training, days upon days of tedious logistical planning, and long hours of old fashioned knuckle-busting work. The expectations were high and forgiveness for failure was nonexistent. The deployment was one of the hardest things I ever accomplished, moving over 1000 soldiers, nearly a hundred armored personnel carriers and scores of wheeled vehicles, on time and in fighting trim when we arrived. The whole deployment took over a month and went smoothly. The 1-18 performed flawlessly during REFORGER.

The early '70s were a turbulent time in our nation. The war in Vietnam was winding down, and racial problems still plagued the country. Many Army units were nearly torn apart by racial strife. These problems did not register on my personal radar, mainly because of the tone Colonel Cavazos set in his brigade. Also, I had a number of fine African-American officers and NCOs who handled racial incidents before they became problems. My S-1 (personnel officer), who was black headed off potentially nasty problems before they reached my desk. In addition, Captain Ben Badie, an outstanding black company commander, who had been a non-commissioned officer in his early career, was my ear to the ground on racial incidents. He had what today would be called "street credibility". When he spoke, the troops, white, black and brown, stopped and listened.

When all else failed, I had God on my side. My battalion chaplain was a Southern Baptist preacher from North Carolina. He stood six-three and weighed 230 pounds with no fat, and had a booming bass voice. If the troops got restless in the barracks, if someone was annoying others with too-loud music, or if an argument looked as if it might escalate, he would suddenly appear and hold an impromptu religious service. Peace and tranquility reigned wherever the chaplain went.

I will not use the chaplain's name, and you will soon see why. When I noticed that he seemed to be in pain, I asked him if anything was wrong. He shyly said yes, and admitted he had a health problem—an enlarged and painful prostate gland. I asked if he had been to the doctor, and he said he had seen our battalion surgeon, who had given him some pills, which apparently were not working. The surgeon also offered a possible explanation for his malady—that his prostate was not being exercised. The chaplain's wife and family were in North Carolina and would remain there until the end of his tour. He confided in me that masturbation was out of the question because it was sinful. And as a devout Christian, any other source of relief was too soul-damning to even consider. After this discussion, which was painfully embarrassing for the chaplain, I had a Solomon-like stroke of wisdom. I called the battalion surgeon and asked him to write a prescription for "Chappie" to masturbate two times weekly. Some weeks later, I asked the chaplain how he was feeling. He grinned and said the pain was entirely gone. God works in mysterious ways, and there is no better job than that of an Infantry battalion commander.

Alas, all good things come to an end. Serving with and working for Colonel Dick Cavazos was just as rewarding at Fort Riley as it had been in Vietnam. I thrived under the pressure and hard work because I knew it was important. The only thing that mattered to me was getting the job done for the "Boss". Cavazos went up the ladder to become the first Hispanic four-star general. His success was achieved through his incredible qualities of intelligence, judgment, character and his amazing capacity for hard work. I love him as much as anyone can love another human being. But it was time for the Boss to be reassigned, and I knew I would probably never get to work for him again.

Atmosphere, morale and spirit de corps in an Infantry unit flow directly from the commander. Good units have good commanders. Hard-luck units are normally led by sub-standard leaders. We had an outstanding brigade because Colonel Cavazos was an outstanding leader. He was replaced by a sub-standard leader.

With only months left in my two-year command tour, I got a new brigade commander. He was a non-Ranger who had served with the 25th Infantry Division in Vietnam. My initial impression was that he was going to be a hard-ass. That was fine with me. I would give him my full measure of support no matter what his personality.

During this time, you, your brother, and your Mom were in Mississippi with your grandparents. Without my family, I devoted my full attention to my soldiers. Breaking in a new brigade commander was very difficult for my staff and company commanders, who were used to the way Colonel Cavazos operated. Things were different under the new brigade commander.

When I was a young officer, I was taught the traits of leadership. Over the years, I have thought about the fourteen traits, and have tried to use them as a guide whenever I was in a leadership position. I could list the traits here, but it would only be a laundry list, so I will dwell only on one of the traits: Loyalty.

Loyalty in the army is meant to go up, down, and sideways. Up meaning that a leader is loyal to his boss, that he can disagree, argue, and give advice, but once the boss makes a decision, the subordinate leader supports him totally. Downward loyalty means that the leader takes care of his subordinates and protects them from unfair treatment. Sideways loyalty means supporting one's peers and fellow leaders to the maximum extent possible. It is easy for a careerist to be loyal to the boss, because lack of loyalty can result in a bad efficiency report. It is also fairly easy to be loyal to friends who command adjacent units. But often, forceful and hard-assed commanders forget how important it is to be loyal to subordinates. And therein lies my story.

One thing that is normally unquestioned in the Army is the necessity to follow the chain of command in all actions and at all times. If something is done that jumps over one link in the chain, the whole thing falls apart. The leader who is bypassed is left in the dark and is unpleasantly surprised when he finds out what is going on. And as you know, I try never to be ambushed.

You, your mother, and Carlton had been visiting your grandparents in Mississippi. It is hard for a battalion commander to find time to take leave, so when your mom was ready to come home, I asked for a weekend pass to go to Columbus to pick all of you up. I was only gone three days. Sunday night, when I returned, my executive officer called and told me that the brigade commander had relieved two of my company commanders. The leadership trait of loyalty and the proper use of the chain of command were being severely tested. I was in the middle of the worst career dilemma I had ever faced. Was I to be loyal to my boss, who had jumped over me in the chain of command, or was I to be loyal to my two young officers whom he had fired? I pondered the situation all night long, but I truly did not comprehend the damage that had been done until I started picking up the pieces the next morning.

If the brigade commander had wanted to fire my two company commanders, all he had to do was to wait until Monday morning. Relieving two of my company commanders while I was gone was completely wrong unless they were in the process of committing an illegal or dangerous act that was detrimental to the welfare of the unit. That was nowhere near the case. He knew it, and I knew it.

I was required by regulations to write Officer Efficiency Reports (OERs) on the two fired officers. Since they had done a fine job for me, I rated them as outstanding. Since he had relieved them, the brigade commander had to write adverse reports on both of them.

When the OERs hit the brigade commander's desk, he called me in.

He said, "Tucker, these guys have been fired. I need you to write relief OERs on them." He was ordering me to change what I had written. I refused to do so.

The loyalty issue had come to a head. The brigade commander had jumped the chain of command and fired two young captains who had done outstanding jobs for me. What should have happened was for the brigade commander to call me in on Monday and say, "Jim, I have a problem with two of your captains who have done thus and so. Let me know how you're going to handle it." This would not have cut me out of the chain and would have allowed me to use my leadership prerogative. Instead, I was being unfairly ordered to adversely rate two fine officers. There was no real decision. I stood loyal to my captains.

Later, I was called to the office of the assistant division commander, who was the reviewer of the OERs.

I walked into his office, saluted and said, "Sir, Lieutenant Colonel Tucker reports as ordered."

The ADC, Red Fuller, said, "Tucker, we've got a problem here".

My response was, "Sir, I don't have a problem". The implication was that it was his problem, not mine. He said he had two irreconcilable efficiency reports that must be reconciled before they were sent forward.

I said, "Sir, I fully understand your dilemma but I cannot add to or delete anything I have written."

"Tucker," he said, "In that case, it is apparent that you're not a team player on this." I understood what he was saying. He had decided to stand with the brigade commander in this most unfair situation. He was asking me to change my outstanding ratings to go along with the derogatory comments the brigade commander had written. I also was fully aware that if I refused, my efficiency report would indicate that I was not a "team player." One little comment like that on an OER would mean that I would never be promoted.

I said, "Sir, I cannot do that. These officers preformed well for me. I have seen nothing that would warrant an adverse OER on either one of them."

He said, "Jim, I hope you know what you're doing."

I saluted, left the office and got into my VW bug. As I drove down Custer Hill from division headquarters I was starkly aware that I had just ended my career. I did not enjoy the remainder of my command time—the atmosphere had been poisoned. When I changed command and departed Fort Riley I received my OER. As I expected, it indicated that I was not a team player.

I have many times since replayed the situation over and over in my mind and have asked myself the question, "If you had it to do over again, would you do anything differently?" The answer always has been "No!" I cannot say that I have not harbored bitterness and animosity toward that brigade commander. No officer should force a subordinate into a career-ending decision in this manner. I believe to this day that the brigade commander simply did not like me or my aggressive style of command. Perhaps he was not impressed by my over abundance of self confidence and wanted to bring me down a notch or two. Since I had done nothing wrong, he had no grounds to fire me, so he concocted the situation with my captains. He just did not have the guts to face me personally, so he relieved my two company commanders during my absence knowing what my reaction would be. The Ranger Curse in action!

A few years ago, after the marina turned out to be successful, and we had become financially comfortable, I called that brigade commander and told him that ending my career was the best thing he could have done for me. The sad thing is that he made brigadier general before being medically retired. I wonder how many other soldiers he treated unfairly along the way.

CHAPTER 12

SAUDI ARABIA

The anguish of having two of my company commanders relieved of their commands while I was hundreds of miles away remains the low point of my twenty-two year career as an Infantryman. The whole episode helped me understand the Japanese tradition of *seppuku*, or ritual suicide. *Seppuku* usually occurred when a samurai warrior felt that his honor had been insulted to the point that he could not live with the resulting embarrassment. Instead of *seppuku*, I dealt with the whole situation by placing it in an emotional lock box with the word "indifference" stenciled on it. Hatred and remorse are emotions that can eat away at one's insides after a while, and I decided not to let this happen to me. By locking away these emotions, I have been able to get on with my life. I once told a psychiatrist friend of mine that I have always survived by being able to laugh and cry at the same time. He replied that he couldn't wait to get me on his couch. I may take him up on his offer when I finish these stories for you.

To add to my frustration and anguish, my next assignment was literally to another world—Saudi Arabia. I left you, your mom and Carlton in Columbus, Mississippi and flew off into another adventure—or so I thought. Having lived in Vietnam for a year, I thought I knew all about culture shock. How wrong I was. Not only were the culture, the religion, the dress and customs drastically different in Saudi Arabia, the terrain looked as if it were on another planet. When I in-processed, I proceeded downward through several layers of bureaucracy until I finally reached the place I would live for the next year. My final destination was in the far southwest part of the country, east of the Red Sea and just north of Yemen, at the city of Khamis Muchayt, 6,500 feet above sea level. At first glance, it didn't look too bad. The low humidity allowed a degree of comfort in the desert heat. The city was more or less what I had come to expect, a mixture of modern times and the sixth century.

What I did not expect however was the military base where I was supposed to be an advisor to the Saudi army. The Saudis had built a multi-million dollar compound with barracks, mess halls, a hospital, an Olympic-sized swimming pool and a state-of-the-art airfield. There were no American soldiers except one artillery officer for me to communicate with. I had no duty except to advise a Saudi colonel on training his troops. I never saw more than 20 troops gathered at one time. The only occupants of this ultra-modern military compound were Bedouin tribesmen who lived in tents and cooked over open fires.

If one had to endure an un-accompanied tour, Khamis Muchayt, at first glance was the ideal place to spend a year. To some, I suppose, life at this place would seem like heaven. As I have said, I live for challenge, adventure, and conflict. Without something to stimulate my adrenal glands, I begin to slowly die inside. Not only was there no stimulation, there was no mission and no troops for me to advise. To me, hell is a place where there is nothing to do, and hell is where I realized I was. But if it was hell, it was a comfortable hell. I wanted for nothing. I was well fed, well housed, and even given a jeep of my own to drive. My only duty appeared to consist of having mid-morning tea with my Saudi colonel. This was the beginning of my second encounter with my demon of boredom, and it looked like this meeting was going to be even more severe than leaving combat in Vietnam to go to school. At least at Leavenworth I had the missions of creating you and passing a test from time to time. Here, I was required to do nothing.

Since I had all the time I needed, I set up a physical training program which became my only reason for existing. My physical regimen allowed me to retain some semblance of sanity, which, I came to later realize, was slowly slipping away. I ultimately ended up running twenty to thirty miles per day, and for the first time in my life, at 40 years of age, was able to do twenty pull-ups. Not since I had attended the British Commando School had I been in such excellent physical condition.

Psychiatrists claim that if a person is crazy, he is unaware of the fact. I found that to be wrong. I knew I was going crazy. To add insult to injury, your mom wrote and told me she was not getting her monthly allotment checks. I didn't know if I was getting paid or not, since I had no need for money—there was nothing to spend it on. Since I was in the middle of nowhere and could not solve the problem, I told your mother to check with the nearest military finance office to see what the problem was. A few weeks later, I opened one of her letters which read, "Tucker, where the hell are you? There is no record of your even being in the Army."

Being sent to Saudi Arabia after battalion command was a sign that my career was not on the fast track, but being dropped from the rolls was a bit extreme. Your grandfather Glover was one of the most astute politicians in Washington. No one ever eclipsed his abilities as a lobbyist. When he died, five presidents sent their condolences. One of his closest friends was Senator John Stennis of Mississippi. I knew that Lorraine knew the senator's secretary. I told your mom to contact her and explain the situation as best she could. In the mean time, I assured her I was in Saudi Arabia and was still in the Army.

Eventually everything got straightened out and I received nearly $4,000 in cash, my share of the four or five months back pay. Your mother also got her back allotment checks. During these months it was apparent to me that much of my mind was not properly functioning. The fact that I had nothing to do and the fact that I missed my family were slowly draining my sanity away. The demon of boredom was trying to take over the sane part of my consciousness, and I knew it was winning.

Staying on the move seemed to help. I would often take my jeep and drive eastward into the famous lost quarter of Saudi Arabia, or I would head west to the Red Sea. As I look back on these trips, I realize now that driving alone through vast stretches of desert probably was not the wisest thing to do. If my jeep had broken down, it might have been days before anyone found me. On one trip, I became acutely aware of the poor judgment I was exercising. As I drove toward the Red Sea, I passed through a sort of canyon, with high banks on each side of the road. As I drove along, I got the feeling someone or something was watching me. I looked up to see that the banks on each side of the road were lined with huge baboons. These creatures were five feet tall and had canine teeth that looked to be two inches long. They stared at me with their human-looking eyes which seemed to ask, "What are you doing in our territory?" If they had attacked, I would have been doomed. That was one of the few times in my life when I did not feel indestructible.

About this time I got a message from my headquarters with instructions to report to Daharan for reassignment to Ryhaid. My new assignment was in the Minister of Defense Office, where officers of all branches and services worked. The simple fact that I now had people to talk to did wonders for my mental state.

The Saudi colonel who was my counterpart spoke English. As I remember, he was a Fort Leavenworth graduate. I enjoyed his companionship and, although alcohol was strictly forbidden in Saudi Arabia, we would sometimes sneak a drink together at my quarters. He and his subordinates seemed to enjoy my company much more when I had scotch whiskey available.

My craziness slowly diminished with the presence of people to interact with. Although it was vastly superior to my existence at Khamis Muchayt, my social life was still what I envisioned life would be like in a monastery. The differences in culture, religion, and language made interaction with Saudi men extremely difficult. And conversing with Saudi females was simply impossible. Dressed in veils and ankle-length robes, they were expressly forbidden to even speak to males who were not members of her immediate family.

This was about the time I met the DeMan family. Vick DeMan was the State Department's agricultural advisor to the Saudis. Vick, Polly and Bruno took me under their care and allowed me to appreciate how much family meant to the stability of human existence. They were lifesavers during a time that I missed my family so much I could taste it.

Near my sixth or seventh month in country I was given an R&R back to the United States. I left Daharan for Frankfurt, Germany, and upon arrival was escorted off the plane and told to report to General George S. Patton, the son of the famous WWII Third Army commander. I have never been intimidated by general officers, but having no idea what the impending meeting was all about, I was somewhat concerned until I realized that in the present stage of my career, there was nothing I should fear.

The next morning, I was taken to a large briefing room where I was directed to meet with General Patton and his staff. As Patton walked in, the only thing that separated him from how I envisioned his father was the fact that he was not wearing ivory-handle revolvers or carrying a swagger stick. He quickly mounted a stage where his staff was arranged in a semi-circle around him. I was suffering the effects of too much gin the night before, and my attitude was, "What the hell can they do to me now other than send me back to Saudi Arabia?" (This was a take-off on the famous Vietnam-era saying, "What can they do to me, send me to Vietnam?")

Toward the end of the meeting, General Patton suddenly said, "We have Lieutenant Colonel Tucker in the audience. He is from Saudi Arabia and works for Colonel Siabe. Maybe he can give us an update on what is going on there."

I had not seen the Saudi colonel or a week or so, and the rumors were that he had taken a Saudi combat brigade to the front and—this was during the 1973 "Yom Kippur War". I remember wondering how the hell he could find the Israeli border because Saudi maps don't even show the country of Israel. Anyway, Patton asked me to brief the assemblage on what I knew about how the Saudis were performing.

I stood and explained, "I don't know much about what is happening. I haven't seen my Saudi boss in a few days. The last reports were that he had been promoted to Brigadier General and had moved his brigade to within hand grenade range of the Israelis."

Now, there is an unspoken rule that in a military briefing to a general officer, jokes are not appropriate. But the insanity of months alone in the desert, and the fact that I knew I didn't have much of a career left anyway, caused me to impulsively add, "The Saudis are throwing hand grenades at the Israelis and the Israelis are pulling the pins and throwing them back."

General Patton, at this point, lost control of himself and so did the audience. He shortly adjourned the briefing and asked me to stand by.

"What now?" I thought! I knew I was probably in trouble.

After a minute or two, General Patton approached me and said "Since I have interrupted your R&R, the least I can do is to take you to dinner."

I accepted. That evening, he and his wife were extremely gracious hosts. General Patton and I would later meet at various Big Red One dinners in Washington where I got to know what a wonderful and engaging person and storyteller he was.

During my R&R, your mom and I met in Washington where she got one of her life-long wishes—to have dinner after one a.m. I recall that also was the night that President Nixon fired his attorney general and two others for not carrying out his orders. At least he understood the chain of command.

During the short time I was in the states, we proceeded to Fort Walton Beach where we had agreed to look for a home. I knew I had no future in the Army and we wanted to retire to the Florida Panhandle. By this time I had 18 years service and retirement was my best option. We drove through several beautiful residential areas looking for the perfect house. On a Saturday morning, after a Friday night made memorable by the number of martinis I consumed, your mom got me up and put me in the back seat of a realtor's car. I was badly hung over so I curled up and dozed as we were taken to look at a house that had been placed on the market the day before. We drove to 590 L'Ombe Court and stopped in the circular driveway. While I was still in the fetal position, your mom got out, looked around and said, "I'll take it"! I never went inside the house before closing the deal, and I don't recall your mom ever going in either. That was the house where you spent your later childhood and teen years. Your mom says that it will be your second home someday.

My return trip to Saudi Arabia, as were all trips into and out of the Middle East, was exciting for me. I boarded the aircraft in New York, flew to England, then to Beirut, Lebanon (which was one of my favorite cities. Back then, in my opinion, it had more class than Paris), where I changed to Saudi Airlines, then made a stop in Damascus. Damascus is one of the oldest cities in the world if I remember my history correctly. Up until the Damascus stop, the plane was filled with beautiful, immaculately dressed and coiffured women wearing the finest smelling perfumes imaginable. It was like traveling inside a Vogue magazine. As soon as the oil fields' gas lights came into view, these ladies disappeared into the rear of the aircraft and returned as veiled specters, clothed head-to-toe in solid black. This transition has to be seen to be fully appreciated.

I used the few remaining months in Ryhaid for planning my future. I knew I was programmed for staff duty at TRADOC (Training and Doctrine Command), at Ft. Monroe, Virginia. I planned to retire after the TRADOC tour. In my conversations with my Saudi co-workers, I had told them of my planned retirement and my wish to go into the business world. They fully understood and cautioned against any business that was related to oil. I never saw a line of vehicles waiting for gasoline in Saudi Arabia, since gas was plentiful and cost only 25 cents per gallon.

I remembered my Saudi friends' warning as I recalled the gas lines in the states in the early '70s.

Since I was going to be stationed in the Tidewater area of coastal Virginia, I decided to do some research sailing, which I had always had a secret interest in. I ordered a copy of an instructional handbook on sailing from the Naval Academy. Inside was a note from the commandant, which I will paraphrase: "You poor bastard. How could I charge a poor bastard serving in Saudi Arabia for a book on sailing. I couldn't possibly charge you. This is on me!"

CHAPTER 13

FROM FORT MONROE
TO HURLBURT

With sailing on my mind, we headed to Hampton, Virginia, where I would become an assistant inspector general in the TRADOC headquarters, where I had some old friends from Vietnam and Fort Benning. An IG officer works directly for the unit commander, in this case a four-star general. As an assistant IG, it was my job to ensure the commander wasn't blindsided by any happening that could cause an embarrassment to the command. Inspectors general investigate wrong doings, breaking of regulations, unlawful acts, and complaints by soldiers. The IG is one of the most important and delicate staff positions that the commander relies on. I did not feel qualified to fulfill this position but my caring for soldiers and appreciating the position of commander was deep in my soul. Little did I know that within three years I would be investigated by this same office.

I did my fair share of the paper shuffling which reinforced my recognition that I was severely lacking in staff skills. I felt sorry for my boss and I will always believe that he came along behind me and cleaned up some of my messes. He never admonished me, even later, when he had the opportunity after we had retired.

I hated the staff work, but I enjoyed the Hampton Rhodes area. Char, you were only three years old, but perhaps you have some memory of our life on Catesby Jones Drive in Hampton, Virginia. A decision I made there changed the direction of our entire lives. Sailing would become the foundation of our lives for the rest of our future. After reading the book on sailing, and of course believing that I could sail as well if not better than anyone else (the Ranger Curse), I convinced your mom that we needed a sail boat. Carlton had taken a sailing course and likely knew more of the basics than did I. I reminded her of what my Saudi buddies had said—get into a business that doesn't require oil. The wind was free but I needed $40,000 to get the boat. She agreed and we soon had a new toy called the "Sweet Obsession". The name came to your mom one night around two a.m. You know she preferred staying up all night and sleeping during the day even back then. Sailing became a family affair as we fully enjoyed the "Sweet Obsession Boat" (SOB). The Chesapeake Bay from Annapolis to Norfolk was a sailor's dream and it soon became our pond.

One day while sailing into Williamsburg, Carlton called to me from the bow, "Daddy, look! That's a Hobie Cat." Two years later I bought the dealership in Fort Walton Beach, and sailing became his life.

While working at my IG job, I discovered there was an assignment for a Lieutenant Colonel of Infantry open at the Air Ground Operations School (AGOS) at Hurlburt Field, Florida. Hurlburt is on the Santa Rosa sound adjacent to Eglin Air Force Base where the Florida Ranger Camp is located. We owned a house in Fort Walton Beach and that assignment was too good to be true. I decided to get that job no matter what the consequences. I went in to discuss this assignment with Lieutenant General Orwin Talbott who had been commander of Fort Benning and the Infantry Center while I commanded the Florida Ranger Camp.

He said, "Tucker, if you proceed to do this you must understand that you will be burning all your bridges behind you."

I said, "Yes, sir, and I fully understand and appreciate your reminding me of the fact."

I had an up on most other people who wanted this job since I had worked for both General William Depuy, the four-star TRADOC commander and his deputy, Lieutenant General Orwin Talbott. I once again asked a general officer for a favor, and it paid off. The only stipulation General Depuy placed on the transfer was that I had to pay for my own move because I had not yet served my full tour at Ft. Monroe. That was one of the most wonderful gestures these two wonderful leaders could give this old Infantryman. I am thankful to this day and I defend them when anyone speaks harshly of them.

I moved all of you to Ft. Walton and returned to Ft. Monroe where I lived on the SOB (Sweet Obsession Boat) so I could close out my assignment there. When I signed out of Fort Monroe, I sailed out of Norfolk in late April and had a wonderful sailing adventure down the Atlantic coast, around the Florida Keys, and across the Gulf of Mexico to Ft. Walton Beach. General Talbott did a part of the trip with me along with Tom Hardy, a family friend, who was the most experienced sailor of all of us. He prevented at least one or two accidents which could have been disastrous. I will leave these stories for another day.

The Air Ground Operations School at Hurlburt was designed to teach the methods for coordinating air support for ground operations.

As the senior instructor on the Army side, I worked for a wonderfully smart and talented Colonel named Jack Whitted. Jack had been a battalion commander in the Big Red One and had worked for General Bill Depuy in Vietnam. During his second Vietnam tour, Jack had the mission of closing out the Army's presence in that tragic little country. Jack often recalled saying goodbye to Vietnam from a C-130 full of bullet holes. Jack was finishing up a 25-plus year career before retiring to his home in Panama City, Florida. Jack was an exceptionally fine infantry officer. During his career he had not only commanded a battalion in combat but had taught at West Point even though he was not a graduate of that institution. He had headed the Airborne Department at Ft. Benning and was recognized by subordinates, peers and seniors as one someone you wanted to serve with. Jack had one negative trait. Veiled by a warm, bubbly outgoing personality was a terrible temper. One did not want to be on the receiving end of one of Jack's explosions. He was a fire plug of a man, all muscle and no fat. He had played college football and had coached at West Point and for teams in the Army. I knew of his reputation before he arrived and had been cautioned not to test his metal, which I wouldn't have anyway because he was a wonderful Infantryman who loved the troops. To me this was a central requirement for being a leader.

Duty in the Army section of the Air Ground Operations School was the easiest duty I had in my career, and that turned out to be a problem. We were teaching students from the mass of knowledge we had gathered during our entire careers. We were Infantry officers who had relied on close air support in combat, and were able to explain first hand the problems and recommended solutions related to the coordination of air and ground power. Since we had to do almost no preparation for classes, the ease of the assignment allowed for complacency and perhaps even a lackadaisical attitude to creep in. I thoroughly enjoyed the assignment and thought there were no ambushes lurking in the bushes. How wrong I was.

My assessment of the Army section's teaching effectiveness was based on the critique sheets that the students filled out at the end of each class. There were never any critical comments about Army instruction. The first hint I had that things weren't going right was from Jack. A new officer had been assigned to the school, and Jack had the feeling he had been sent there to check up on the Army section. In my mind, I dismissed that possibility because the new officer was a Citadel classmate. I believed that if he had been given the task of spying on us, he would have told me. Some weeks later, an IG team showed up to evaluate complaints about the Army Section. Jack and I were specifically mentioned in the complaint. I was not overly concerned because I knew we were getting the job done.

There were seven Army officers working for me. There was a rumor that two of them were unhappy with the amount of time Jack and I spent in our offices. The amount of time the Army section worked in our offices was my decision and I was prepared to defend myself in this regard. One thing that no doubt affected Army officers' perceptions was the fact that I had recently bought the Hobie Cat dealership in Fort Walton and often spent time there during afternoons and evenings after work. It was a fact that I did not take lunch and sometimes left the office early. I was not concerned about this since all work was being done and all requirements were being met.

The IG team interviewed all the Army officers and a number of Air Force officers and enlisted personnel. I later found out through the Freedom of Information Act that one of the complaints against me was that I had forced an Air Force NCO into buying a Hobie Cat. Just the opposite was true. He came to me and asked to buy one and I sold it to him at dealer cost. The report's final conclusion seemed to indicate that there was not sufficient supervision provided to the Army instructors and that corrective action should take place.

A few weeks after the IG team departed, Jack and I were ordered to come to Ft. Monroe for a meeting with our boss, a two star that I had never met. Jack went into his office first and after ten minutes or so came out and said he had been fired and was going to retire. I knew he was going to retire, but the way this was coming down really angered me, and my adrenalin was starting to flow. When it was my turn, I went in, saluted and reported. I was told to take a seat in an overstuffed chair that was so low to the floor that it put me in a near squatting position, well below the general's level. He got straight to the point by offering me immediate retirement or an Article 15 (non-judicial punishment). At this point in my career, an Article 15 would have been less than a hand slap to me—but my pride was on the line. I told him in no uncertain terms that retirement was out of the question even though I had finished 20 years which would allow me a pension. The idea that he was trying to dictate to me how I would end my career was beyond my comprehension, particularly since there had been no real charges against me. As my temper flared, I accented my statements by pounding my fist on the floor. I firmly refused an Article 15 and demanded a trial by court martial, which was my right. I had called his bluff. He and I both knew I didn't have to accept an Article 15 and could demand court martial. He and I also I knew there were no charges under UCMJ that could or would allow me to be found guilty of anything. He said I would be hearing from him and he dismissed me. I never heard from him again.

Jack and I returned to AGOS and a month or so later he retired. I was heart broken and wounded by what I had let happen to my boss. It was my job to protect him and I failed. He took it all in his normal jocular accepting way—the way Infantrymen learn to accept life as it is thrown at them. I have never accepted his forced retirement. To this day I wish I could have prevented him from being forced to retire. I stayed on at AGOS and settled for some revenge. The Air Force colonel got in trouble for improperly using government travel funds. I wrote two of the officers who worked for me and were, in my opinion, a part of the conspiracy, OERs which would insure they were never promoted. I was told they contested these efficiency reports but were not successful. As for the Judas who started the whole thing, his identity is still unknown to all but me.

In my remaining time in service I stayed at AGOS and discovered some of the underlying causes for the conspiracy between some of my Army officers and the AGOS staff. It boiled down to inter-service rivalry and parochialism. It seems the AGOS commandant and his staff felt the Air Force would never be able to move ahead in their quest to control more of the land battle if officers like Jack Whitted and I were there to prevent even the slightest encroachment into land battle. Jack and the AGOS commandant would sometimes spar over the different rolls of air support in front of their staff members. There was growing resentment over the term "acting in support of". I was once informed by an Air Force colonel that he was tired of always being "in support like a jockey strap".

My response was simple: "Then, sir, you should change the color of your uniform." The conflict between the Army's and the Air Force's concept of air-ground operations continued for years. This lack of cooperation was made painfully evident when we went into Grenada. Hardly anyone in the air could talk to anyone on the ground. Some lessons were learned and applied when we went into Panama, but the problem still had not been solved. It was not until Desert Storm when the Army, Air Force and Navy began to effectively coordinate air support for ground operations. This was due in part to the leadership of General Chuck Horner, the Air Component Commander working for Schwarzkoph. Our incursion into Afghanistan in 2001 demonstrated how far we have come. The Air Force provided outstanding air support for our special operations troops. In fact, Special Forces teams working with Northern Alliance soldiers were able to use laser and GPS guided bombs dropped from B-52s flying at 30,000 feet as close air support. This combination of counterinsurgency strategy combined with smart weapons defeated the Taliban in a short time.

Iraq was a different story. Fear of collateral damage drove commanders to place extremely restrictive rules of engagement on both ground and air assets. Air power, however, was a tremendous help in the 3rd Infantry Division's dash to Baghdad, but still, problems remain.

Hopefully many of the problems we had in Vietnam and at the Air Ground Operations School have been solved. Evidence of new inter-service cooperation is the fact that the Armed Forces Staff College at Norfolk, Virginia, has been renamed to the Joint Forces Staff College. There, officers from all services are schooled in joint operations. Despite the giant strides that have been made, I believe the ultimate solution is for the close air support assets of the Air Force to be brought into the Army. Once that happens we can enjoy the full advantages that close air support can bring to the land battle. Until then, inter-service rivalries and parochialism will continue to plague the air-ground war. I believe that unless the Army and Air Force cooperate as the Special Operations Wing did with our Rangers during our training mission in Florida, we will struggle along missing the opportunities to once again win a war!

Our family has a long history dealing with the issue of air power. Your grandfather was an Army officer who flew with Eddie Rickenbacker in the 94th Aero Squadron. He was an Ace with the "Hat and Ring" squadron, and earned the Distinguished Service Cross and the Croix de Guerre—The Cross of War—in 1917. A photograph of the last gathering of the Squadron at the Waldorf in 1919 hangs in our upstairs hallway. Sometimes you should take my grandchildren out to Columbus Air Force Base, known as Kaye Air Force Base from 1941-1947, and show them "Kaye Auditorium". Both were named for your grandfather. It is a proud heritage that flows in your veins.

Determined to leave the Army under my terms, I chose the time of retirement to be at midnight on 31 December, 1978, for no reason except that hopefully I could remember it. The morning of 1 January 1979 was like most other mornings. I got up and went to work doing the things I enjoyed. I have been able to do that most of my life and I am still doing so.

It seems that after all those years, my battles are not over yet. Perhaps I'm always looking for a cause or a fight. Remember the cocktail party at the Bid Red One's annual reunion? If you recall, the chairman of the dinner came up to me and said I could not take you into the formal dinner with me even though I had purchased a ticket for you. The reason he gave was the fact that you are my daughter and not my son. (It had been a long-standing tradition that only combat officers and their sons may attend the dinner.) I hope you didn't hear me tell him to "get fucked and get out of my face". But I guess you realize that coming from me that wouldn't be a much of a shock.

Earlier this year, I sent an e-mail to the 1st Battalion 18th Infantry representative stating that if the upcoming reunion in 2010 is to be the last in Washington, you would be attending as my *aide-de-camp*. After he "ran it up the flag pole", he informed me that the powers-that-be didn't want to break tradition and provide you a ticket. Sons were okay as ticketed guests, but not daughters. If that is their final word—and I don't think it will be—then we will be going to the reunion and they will have to physically prevent our being seated at the dinner.

I guess I always need some stress in my life, and if it does not come along in the normal course of events, I seem to go looking for it. Controversy, unusual happenings, and weird and crazy events seem to seek me out.

Transitioning from the Army into civilian life was traumatic to say the least. I brought my fighting spirit with me into retirement. After I retired and tried to get started in business, I had to sue Hobie Cat just to get them to let me sell their product. I made the statement to them that what's good for me is good for Hobie Cat and that's good for the country. I won the lawsuit!

I entered the business world in Fort Walton Beach as a babe in the woods. I thought I had left the dangerous world of combat behind me. Instead, I found the business world replete with ambushes, minefields and snipers. It took me some time, perhaps too long, to realize that there are many similarities between jungle fighting and combat in the civilian business arena. The tactics are different, but the principles still apply.

For example, leadership is leadership, no matter what the situation or the people involved. In business I found myself leading about ten people instead of a thousand. I brought with me into retirement the leadership lessons I had learned by experience and at the feet of masters. For example, communication in the civilian world is vastly different from I had practiced in the Army. I found that Army style communication works extremely well with civilian workers. All that is required is to give them clear, concise instructions and follow up with supervision that does not get in their way. As in the military, the most important thing in civilian leadership is to convey your intent to your workers without alienating them. I found that teamwork is nonexistent in the civilian world unless you purposely build it—and you build it by treating people right. Once you build a team, morale and productivity increase exponentially.

I thought I would never have to use my knowledge of tactics once I retired. How wrong I was. In tactics, the leader uses maneuver to seize his objective. In business, the objective is making money. I had no idea of the resistance and cunning that the bureaucracies and competitors (the enemy) had awaiting me. I had to learn new tactics and I had to learn them quickly.

I learned that the firepower I had always relied on in the Army had a parallel in business. Money, capital, lines of credit and borrowing power are the big guns in the civilian world. Just as I had Dick Cavazos to teach me combat tactics and the use of firepower, I had Al Qualls to protect me from civilian ambushes. Al is a Fort Walton Beach banker who has been a friend and mentor for 30 years. Not only has he guided me through many complicated transactions, he is also a huge supporter of the Florida Ranger Camp.

Charlotte, when you read this, my last days as an old Infantryman will not have fully played out. I am fighting one more battle—to have daughters attend our reunion dinner. The First Infantry Division Reunion Dinner Committee has refused to allow you or any other daughter to attend. Sons will continue to be allowed. I mention this because a decade from now no one will believe this position by the dinner committee. But you and I will because we were there.

In 2011 the Combat Officers' Dinner Committee voted to allow daughters the same privileges as sons to attend the formal dinner with their fathers. Because of our efforts, a 94-year-old tradition finally ended.

CHAPTER 14

WILTON "PAPPY" WHITE

The reason I am telling this story about Pappy White is to clear up an issue that has been haunting me for years. Pappy White was a unique Ranger instructor. When a Ranger student asked Pappy what Ranger school was like back when he went through, Pappy replied, "I never went to Ranger school". The student then asked, "Then how did you get the Ranger tab?" Pappy answered, "By lying next to a trail watching the Japanese walk by."

Pappy White was a World War II veteran of the Sixth Ranger Battalion, which fought in the Pacific theater of war. He was also a veteran of the Vietnam War, having served as a platoon sergeant in the 18th Infantry (my old unit) of the First Infantry Division. Despite his age, Pappy did everything the younger instructors did. The average age of my officer instructors was less than twenty-five, and they were delighted to find themselves working with a WWII Ranger who was twenty years their senior, thus the nickname "Pappy". We had all fought the Viet Cong, but Pappy had also fought the Japanese and lived to tell about it. He was a hero to all of us.

No Ranger officer ever complained about having Pappy walk a patrol as his assistant evaluator. Pappy's instruction to Ranger students was always quiet, patient, and full of detail that only a veteran with a great number of years can call forth. Throughout the years, I have discussed Pappy's performance with colonels and four-star generals. Not one of them ever spoke a negative word about him. I wish I could have that said of me!

When I assumed command of the Florida Ranger Camp, I became aware that Pappy was a member of the WWII Ranger Association. When he told me of an upcoming meeting of the group at Cape Canaveral, I asked if he could get me an invitation along with a few minutes of podium time. At the meeting, old Rangers were full of wine, war stories, and great affection for each other. I was envious of the comradeship and love they shared. When I was introduced as the commander of the Florida Ranger Camp, I was warmly accepted as one of them, although most of them had no idea about what modern Ranger training was all about. I briefly explained the training and what was required to achieve the Ranger Tab. I supposed that these Darby's Rangers and the men who had climbed the cliffs at Pointe du Hoc, having faced what they had, were very aware of their own mortality. With the belief that they would want their heritage carried on after they had gone, I recommended they allow modern Rangers to join their association.

After my briefing, I asked for comments or questions. There were a few tentative and polite questions, then from the back of the room came a booming voice with a definite Yankee accent. "Colonel", the old Ranger bellowed, "Why should my fellow Rangers and I allow you and your group of fellow Rangers, who can't even whip a group of black-pajama clad farmers, into our organization?" I was not prepared for such a question and I'm sure I stammered a weak answer.

Pappy heard the entire exchange and fully understood his buddies' reluctance. That's when Pappy went to work. In his quiet way, he explained to the group that he had fought the Japanese as well as the Viet Cong, and that in his experience, the VC were every bit the soldiers the Japanese were. The fact that Pappy was the only member of the organization who represented both the WWII veterans and the modern Rangers was not lost on the assemblage. Pappy very adroitly painted a picture that brought the two generations of Rangers together.

When the reunion was over, Pappy and I returned to work at the Ranger camp. After the emotionally charged question the old Ranger had asked me, my pride was damaged and I felt we were fighting a losing battle. But Pappy assured me that things would work out. He asked my permission to invite his association's members to the Ranger camp to observe our training. I readily agreed, and the old Rangers came to watch our students as they underwent the rigors of the Florida phase. In the end, due to Pappy's hard work, my dream of a combined U.S. Army Ranger

Association (USARA) was realized. When the list of original members was compiled, Pappy's name was near the top and I was assigned the number 00034. My friend Al Qualls was instrumental in financing the association's startup. Although it got off to a sputtering beginning, the association grew rapidly. Future Ranger Tab wearers would now be able to trace their linage back to their WWII roots.

After my retirement, (Retired Major General) Ken Leuer and I were reminiscing about our youthful deeds when he suggested I recommend Pappy for the Ranger Hall of Fame. I was embarrassed that I had not thought about this idea, but Ken was always ahead of me. I wrote the recommendation and included letters from senior officers such as Hugh Shelton who had walked patrols with Pappy. The recommendation included the fact that Pappy had participated in the famous Cabanatuan raid in the Philippines, which rescued 511 American POWs miles behind Japanese lines. All of us who had worked with Pappy were delighted when he was inducted into the hall of fame. He cherished the honor.

As the Ranger Association grew in numbers and more WWII Rangers participated in reunions, and books and articles were published, there was a growing chorus from the veterans of the Sixth Ranger Battalion that Pappy had not been on the legendary operation. The raid on the POW camp at Cabanatuan, was conducted by C Company and a platoon from F Company, Sixth Ranger Battalion. During this controversy, I argued that whether or not he had been on the raid, my principal reasons for recommending Pappy for the Hall of Fame were his outstanding service as a Ranger instructor and his efforts in establishing the U.S. Army Ranger Association. But the questions persisted. I knew then as I know now that Army rosters, particularly in combat, are often incomplete or inaccurate. In addition, almost no Army operation is conducted by a "pure" unit. There are always attachments such as artillery forward observers, communications personnel, medics and other strap hangers. In fact, during the Cabanatuan raid, a detachment of signal corps camera men went along to record the action. Also, Alamo Scouts and Philippine guerrillas were attached. The fact that Pappy was not on a C or F Company roster is not, in my opinion, necessarily evidence of anything—he could have been an attachment. The length of time since WWII, Army record keeping, and the fog of war make disputing the recollections and claims of a fine old Infantryman an exercise in futility. But that did not convince Pappy's detractors. The USARA removed him from the Ranger Hall of Fame.

Pappy retired in 1971 after 30 years of service. Shortly before his death in 2003, Pappy and his wife and family came to visit me. Pappy did not look well and I suspected it might be our last meeting. He said the reason for his visit was to assure me that he had not deceived me or anyone else about his WWII service. He said, "Colonel Tucker, I swear I was there!" I told Pappy I believed him. As far as I was concerned his was a deathbed confession. We embraced and said goodbye. A few weeks later I saw him for the last time. He was in his casket. No good deed goes unpunished.

Over the past few years, there have been a number of Rangers who have questioned the removal of Pappy from the RHOF. I hope that Pappy will soon be reinstated. It is the right thing to do. Without his hard work and loyalty, there would be no United States Army Ranger Association.

EPILOGUE

I am writing this memoir so that someday, if my grandchildren want to know what grandpa did during his life, they will have something to refer to. The stories I have told may give hints at what makes me tick, but they are not the whole story. I thought I would state a little bit of my view of world events. It might be interesting for them, many years in the future, to see how right or wrong I was.

I no longer have a voice in what happens within our military. Since my retirement from the Army, I have only discussed my philosophy of war with those who have directly participated in combat at battalion level or lower. Discussing war with someone who has not experienced the shock of battle is like a woman trying to describe childbirth to a man. For 30 years, I have largely remained silent while watching and reflecting on our nation's use of our military to further our national interests. Now that I am an old man, and as our nation teeters on the edge of widening a 9-year long war in Afghanistan, old feelings surface, and I feel I must philosophize. For the first time I will divulge my feelings to those who have not experienced war.

As in Vietnam, we are again involved in a conflict that has religious, tribal, and territorial aspects, and are fighting in an area where there are no front lines and it is difficult to ascertain who the enemy is. While I agree with the objective of defeating terrorism, I fear for our military people, particularly the Infantrymen, both Army and Marine, because they are mainly the ones who will do the dying. Our young people will accomplish any mission given them, but they must have a clear objective. Colonel Harry Summers wrote that by 1967, U.S. officials had stated over 20 statements of objective in Vietnam. We accomplished none of these. We cannot make that same mistake in Afghanistan. I fear that if we establish an objective in Afghanistan of pacifying, building and establishing a stable government, we will fail as we did in Vietnam. To date, I have heard no statement of objective in Afghanistan from the president or secretary of defense. Nation building is beyond the capability of the Infantryman, so the complete power of our nation must be brought to bear, and I feel it will not be.

I go back to what I have stated before. Since Vietnam, I have believed that commanders should fight with fire power, not human bodies. The enemy in Afghanistan is a heartless bastard. He hides among helpless civilians, daring us to use our overwhelming firepower. He knows if we do, and if civilians are killed, he has a tool he can use to whip up angst against the U.S. I fear that in Afghanistan, high-level commanders fearing collateral damage will play right into the Taliban's hands. Fear of civilian casualties will cause our leaders to establish restrictive rules of engagement which will end up requiring rifle-to-rifle combat by our Infantry. This is the exact opposite of what I have always believed. I believe in throwing everything at the enemy except the bodies of our soldiers. If an Infantryman is given a mission, he will accomplish it no matter what. He sees no wiggle room, no excuse for failing to accomplishing his mission. But if our Infantrymen are given unrealistic missions to accomplish without the benefit of all the supporting fires we have available, too many will die. If we are not going to use all means to avoid man-to-man combat, I warn the commander-in-chief, just as I warned George Tronsrue: "Don't go in there. It's an ambush!"

BOOK TWO

THE FLORIDA RANGER CAMP

By Lieutenant Colonel (Retired) John E. Gross

Charlotte, I have met you twice, once when Tucker was inducted into the Ranger Hall of Fame as a Distinguished Member of The Ranger Training Brigade. The other time was at your parents' birthday party in October, 2009. Your mother was pregnant with you when I served with Tucker at the Florida Ranger Camp, so I know that you couldn't know anything of what he accomplished there. I am honored to be allowed to help tell his story.

During my 22 year career, I worked for or with 15 lieutenant colonel battalion commanders. They were all different. Some were smart, some were not so smart, some were honest, some were less than honest, some were politicians and some were field soldiers, some were decent men and others were outright SOBs.

When I came home from Vietnam and was assigned to the Florida Ranger Camp as an instructor, I was a captain with two and a half years in the Army. Up until that point, I had worked for four battalion commanders—two in the 82nd Airborne Division and two in the 9th Division in Vietnam. These men were light years away from me in terms of age and experience. Mostly I had respect for them, but I held them in awe, and was a little nervous in their presence. At that time, the image I had in my mind of a lieutenant colonel commander was that of an aloof, middle-aged, distant, demanding, hard-ass, with very little sense of humor.

And then came Tucker. When he arrived in Florida, he was still a major, but was quickly promoted. After two promotions ahead of his contemporaries, at 35 he was the youngest lieutenant colonel in the Army. The first thing that struck me was his youthfulness. A far cry from the middle-aged battalion commanders I had known, he looked as young as we were. With his rock-hard physique and shiny bald head, he was a striking figure. Behind his back, we all called him Mr. Clean. He looked just like the figure on the Mr. Clean detergent bottle.

The first thing he did when he assumed command of the Florida Ranger Camp was to announce that we would have an officers' call, and the uniform would be shorts and running shoes. He led us on a two-mile run, after which we returned to the officers' club for Bloody Maries. He didn't scold anyone who lagged behind. He didn't make a speech. All he had done was to put us on notice that he expected his officers to be in top physical condition.

There was a belief among captains in the Army at that time that a battalion commander was either a politician, who spent his time trying to make a good impression on the generals, or a tactician who was at home in the field with soldiers. Most young captains quickly sized up new commanders as either politicians or tacticians (of course, we preferred the tacticians). We believed that no officer could be both at the same time. Tucker was both. He seemingly knew every general in the Army, and did not hesitate to pick up the phone to ask them for what he wanted. What impressed us about Tucker was that he was not the least bit concerned about trying to impress anyone, regardless of his rank. He had the self confidence to simply say what he thought and was willing to let the chips fall where they may. Tucker was also extremely proficient as a field soldier, a natural when it came to the business of being a Ranger. His service under Dick Cavazos gave him knowledge and experience as a combat operations officer that far surpassed almost all of his contemporaries.

There was another old Army adage that the commander should not be friends with his subordinates; that the commander should maintain a certain distance between himself and those he commanded. Not Tucker. We knew he was the commander, but he was one of us too. He was a friend we could talk to. He had a quick temper, but after blowing up, he would calm down quickly and he never held a grudge. He could out-run every one of us (except Captain Mike Burton), he could beat us all at arm wrestling, and could drink us all under the table. His approach to leadership was to simply assume we were all experienced combat veterans who were there to get the job done. He knew that all he had to do was point us in the right direction and that we would accomplish the mission or die trying.

Tucker established an atmosphere at the Florida Ranger Camp that freed all of us from worrying about our efficiency reports or our careers. We knew instinctively that he would take care of us, and he knew we would do anything he asked, without question. This atmosphere fostered a fierce loyalty between Tucker and his Ranger instructors. He never had to reprimand us. All he had to do was act a little disappointed in us and we felt worse than having had our asses royally chewed.

He listened to all of us equally, no matter what our rank. Once in a pre-cycle meeting, the subject of walking on trails came up. The Ranger policy was that patrols never walked on roads and trails because of the danger of enemy ambushes, booby traps and mines. As usual, Tucker opened the discussion to all, officer and NCO alike. Some officers who had served in the central highlands in Vietnam claimed that the terrain had forced them to patrol on trails and we ought to teach our students how to do it. SFC Eddie Sutton, a huge bear of a man, surprised everyone by suddenly jumping up and storming from the room. He returned minutes later with a Life magazine, which he opened to a double-page color photograph of a pile of American soldiers lying dead on a trail. He shouted, "This is what happens when you walk on trails! This is what happened to my company."

Tucker simply said, "Next topic."

In 22 years, I served with a lot of soldiers, and I remained in contact with very few of them. But I know where my Ranger buddies are, and we stay in touch. Why? Because of the special time at the Florida Ranger Camp working for Tucker. It was a magic time. Those two years were a serendipitous collision of the right time, the right place, the right people, the right mission, the right commander, and a lot of testosterone. All of Tucker's Ranger instructors were Vietnam combat veterans. All of us had had the same experience when we returned from Vietnam. We had been pulled from the jungle, put on a plane, and landed back in our country, far removed in distance and understanding from Southeast Asia. Many of us were still suffering from the effects of close combat when we returned to our loved ones, who had no concept of what was going on in our minds.

At the Florida Ranger Camp, our classrooms were the coastal swamps and pine forests of the Florida panhandle. We had the mission to teach young leaders how to survive in the jungles of Vietnam and keep their soldiers alive. Our daily duties became a salve to our souls as we shared our combat experiences with Ranger students during endless patrols. As we taught our students the tactics they would need in Vietnam, we talked the war out of our systems. Also, over C-ration meals under the pines, or under the wings of airplanes as we waited for parachute jumps, or during breaks in instruction, we opened our hearts and nightmares to our fellow Ranger instructors. At the Ranger camp, we were afforded an opportunity that few returnees had. The camp became the venue for a sort of swamp therapy as we came down slowly from the trauma of close combat. As we did our jobs, we healed ourselves and each other. We became close to each other, and we became close to Tucker. And it has remained that way for over 40 years.

The number of Tucker's captains and majors who made general is one indication of how special the officers who served with him were. When Hugh Shelton was promoted to major, Tucker told him, "You might make general if you learn to smile." Shelton became Chairman of the Joint Chiefs of Staff. Captain John Lemoyne, the camp S-1, rose to command Fort Benning as a Major General and later became Deputy Chief of Staff for Personnel for the entire Army as a Lieutenant General. Major Bob Frix, the camp XO was promoted to Major General, and was installed (as was Tucker) as a Distinguished Member of the Ranger Training Brigade, part of the Ranger Hall of Fame. At a Ranger reunion in 2001, General Hugh Shelton pointed at Tucker and said, "No matter how many stars I have, there is my commander!"

Charlotte, one of the things I am proudest of in my career, is the simple fact that I was one of Tucker's captains. I will now tell you some stories about your dad as our Ranger commander. I hope you enjoy them. They are all true.

CARLTON AND THE ROPE DROP

There are two confidence tests that must be negotiated by Ranger students before they are awarded the Ranger Tab. These tests are designed to help them overcome their natural fears of height and water.

At the end of the Benning phase, students underwent an all-night escape and evasion exercise that ended at Victory Pond. After breakfast, the Rangers had to zip down the Slide-For-Life and negotiate the Rope Drop. The Slide-For-Life consisted of a half-inch steel cable attached to the top of an 80-foot tower. The other end of the cable was fastened to a point in the water about 80 yards away. Ranger students had to climb the tower, attach a pulley with a handle on it to the cable, then lift their feet from the platform, causing the pulley to roll down the cable until the student reached the speed of about 50 miles per hour. When an instructor dropped a signal flag, the student released the handle and splashed into the water.

The second confidence test was known as the Rope Drop. Three 40-foot telephone poles set vertically in the water about 30 feet apart formed the base of the apparatus. Another telephone pole was bolted across the top of two of the vertical poles. A 2" X 8" board was nailed to the top of the horizontal pole, forming a narrow walkway. In the middle of the horizontal structure were two boxes, one atop the other forming a set of steps. A rope extended from the far pole to another pole about 30 feet out in deeper water. Centered on the rope was a large wooden Ranger Tab. To negotiate the obstacle, a Ranger student had to climb up the first pole using attached steel rungs. He then had to walk upright across the walkway, up and down the two steps to the rope. He then had to swing under the rope and monkey-crawl to the Ranger Tab. After touching the wooden tab, he lowered his body so that he was hanging vertically from the rope. He would then ask permission from the instructor to drop. The Ranger instructor would yell, "Look at the sky!" and then "Drop!" The student would scream "RAN-GERRRRR!" until he splashed into the water.

For some unknown reason, Tucker thought it would be great for one of the confidence tests to be done at the end of the Florida phase, right before graduation. Just east of the camp was a large pond that was deep enough, so Tucker requisitioned help from Air Force engineers to build a Rope Drop. Before the training schedule could be changed so the Rope Drop came at the end of the course, Tucker had to get the blessing of the Ranger Department director. Colonel John Geraci had only one question for Tucker: "Is it safe?"

Tucker replied, "Hell yes! As a matter of fact, the first person to go off of it will be my nine-year-old son!"

When the Ranger Camp was moved from Field 7 to Field 6 early in Tucker's command tour, quarters became available at the camp, and that is where the Tuckers lived. The Florida Ranger Camp must have been a wondrous place for a nine-year-old boy. There were guns, helicopters, parachute jumps, snakes and alligators. When Carlton Tucker was not in school, he wandered about the camp and became sort of a mascot. He was into everything his father would let him get into. Sometimes he had to be shooed away from training.

When the engineers had completed the Rope Drop, Tucker immediately wanted it tested. He decided to christen his new training device by having all instructors in the camp negotiate the obstacle. The rope had not been installed yet, so Rangers had to climb the pole, cross the walkway, step up and down the steps, then jump off the far side.

True to his word, Tucker summoned Carlton to be the first jumper. He told me to go up to take care of Carlton and to insure that he jumped.

In 1991, while I was visiting Tucker at his marina in Fort Walton Beach, Carlton said that he remembered me. He said, "You were the one that threw me off the Rope Drop!"

I remembered it differently.

Carlton was first to climb the pole. I followed close behind him. At the top, he extended his arms for balance and slowly and carefully walked across the narrow board. He paused a second or two at the steps, but he made it over. When he reached the end of the walkway, he turned and looked at me.

"JUMP", cried Tucker from below.

Carlton looked at me with eyes as big as saucers, then looked down at the water.

"JUMP!" yelled Tucker.

"There's no going back." I told him. "Look, someone else has climbed the pole and is on the walkway. There's no way down but to jump."

"JUMP, CARLTON!" screamed Tucker, his face turning red.

Carlton looked at me, then at the water.

"You can do it." I said.

He looked at me again, at his father, then at the water. Without another word, he launched into space. His small body hardly made a splash when he hit the water. When he surfaced, he looked up at me and grinned. Like the big boys, like the Rangers, he had met his fears and conquered them. I gave him a thumbs up.

Then I had a great idea. My Ranger blood was up and I decided not just to do a normal jump. I stood for a moment going over my dive in my mind. Tucker must have thought I was hesitating.

"JUMP, GROSS!"

"Just a minute, I'm thinking," I said.

"JUMP, DAMMIT!"

I pushed off the pole, threw my head back and did a perfect back flip, splashing down on my feet. That did it. Almost every Ranger behind me tried some kind of special jump. There were dives, cannonballs, can-openers, and flips. Some were successful and some weren't, some ending in spectacular and painful splashes. On my second jump, I tried a front one-and-a-half and landed on my back, knocking the wind out of me. When Major Bob Frix came across the walkway and crossed the steps, he took off in a dead run toward the end of the board and launched into a perfect swan dive. Because we were who we were, one jump was not enough. Rangers climbed, jumped, flipped and dived until Tucker called a halt.

As we walked up the hill back to the camp, Carlton danced along beside Tucker, gesticulating with his hands as he retold the story of his jump over and over.

And I swear I did NOT throw him off!

Carlton Tucker died of a heart attack in 1998.

DEATH OF THE BLUES

The dining-in is a treasured tradition in the U.S. Army. There are several explanations as to the origin of the dining-in. Most state that the tradition derives from British regiments stationed overseas in the colonies. Without the comfort of their wives and families who remained in England, the officers gathered in the "mess" for dinner on a regular basis. Whether in a fine dining room with crystal or silver, or in a tent where dinner was served in mess kits, the officers of the regiment joined together for bonding and camaraderie.

Dinner was a time to socialize new officers, good-naturedly rib comrades, and to blow off steam. The evening's festivities were overseen by the regimental colonel, who acted as president of the mess. The junior officer had the duty of being "Mr. Vice". No one could speak to the president of the mess without obtaining permission from Mr. Vice. If an officer was caught committing an etiquette faux pas, he was challenged with a "point of order". The charging officer would state, "Mr. Vice, a point of order, please." The accuser would then state the offense to the president of the mess who would assess a fine against the perpetrator. It was good-natured fun and it taught manners and regimental traditions to new officers. Following the formal dinner, there would be an informal time when officers played cards or chess, or sat and talked over brandy and cigars. Sometime in history, the dining-in became a tradition in the U.S. Army—and it became Americanized.

Things are different in our military today from the way they were during the Vietnam War. Alcohol is being de-glamorized, and life on an Army post has become more family oriented than it was then. In short, the officer corps is more civilized today than it was during Vietnam.

During that era, Army officers could look forward to maybe a year in the states between Vietnam tours, and as support for the war waned, the give-a-shit factor became less evident. In fact, some officers' clubs more closely resembled saloons in Dodge City in 1880 than gathering places for officers and gentlemen on an Army post. If an officer received a rebuke or chastisement during those days, his answer was normally, "What are they going to do, send me to Vietnam?" If modern-day officers did some of the things we did in the late '60s, they would go directly to jail or immediately be drummed out of the Army.

During the Vietnam era, a dining-in (which is a stag affair) at Fort Bragg or Fort Riley was liable to be a rowdy event. But a dining-in at the Florida Ranger Camp usually turned out to be an orgy of debauchery. Besides being 200 miles from higher Army headquarters, the camp was located 25 miles from the headquarters of Eglin Air Force Base. Being located in the middle of nowhere gave the Rangers the feeling that no one was watching—a potentially dangerous situation for strong and fit young men who thought themselves to be bullet proof.

The American Army version of the dining-in consisted of posting of the colors, an invocation, toasts, Mr. Vice's sampling of the food to see if was "suitable for human consumption", then dinner. During the meal, points of order were offered and fines were assessed. Payment for some fines was physical in nature. Doing pushups or low-crawling in dress blues were routine punishments for such things as talking with a full mouth, or putting one's elbows on the table. The meal was followed by remarks from a guest speaker and retirement of the colors. When the color guard exited the room, the president of the mess then announced, "Gentlemen, the smoking lamp is lit!" This was the signal for the informal portion of the evening to begin.

At a Florida Ranger Camp dining-in, the lighting of the smoking lamp was the signal for all hell to break loose. At one dining-in, Ranger officers ate a six-foot rubber tree, placed a Ranger decal on the 20-foot ceiling of the Hurlburt officers' club by building a human pyramid in their dress blues, and drank punch from a bowl in which was a frozen rattlesnake. At one dining-in at the Eglin main officers club, a piglet was brought into the mess with the words "East Bay Hog" written on its sides with magic marker. (This was in relation to a rumor of a gigantic wild boar several Rangers said they had seen in the East Bay Swamp. The hog got bigger and bigger with each telling.) The piglet escaped and ran squealing through the main dining room with Ranger officers in dress blues merrily chasing after it. Following that dining-in, the Commanding General of Eglin Air Force Base had words with the Commander, Florida Ranger Camp. The next night, the Eglin club burned to the ground, and of course the Rangers were suspected of arson. Only when fire investigators stated the fire was caused by an electrical short did everyone breathe a little easier.

At another dining-in, a Ranger captain walked into the mess wearing an Air Force full colonel's flight suit. When asked where he got it, he said, "I found it". Then an older gentleman, obviously inebriated, wandered in to the mess in his underwear. He was promptly offered a drink, which he accepted and joined the festivities.

At Tucker's first dining-in as camp commander, he offered to arm wrestle every officer in the room. He did and beat them each one in turn. Major Bob Frix, camp XO, offered to fist fight anyone in the room. He went around offering his chin and saying, "Go ahead, take your best shot!" One captain took up the offer and nailed him. Frix shook off the punch and wandered off in search of further confrontation.

But it was Tucker's last dining in that became a legend within the Rangers. It was at this event that Major Bob Frix announced that he was going swimming. He went out to the pier behind the club, stripped to his shorts, then sprinted toward Santa Rosa Sound. What he did not realize was that the tide was out. He did a beautiful swan dive, spattering in the mud and slicing his chest open in many places by sea shells.

Near the end of a rough and rowdy informal portion of the evening, Tucker looked down and proclaimed, "Look at my dress blues—THEY'RE RUINED!" He then ordered the assemblage outside, where he removed his uniform, tacked it to an oak tree, doused it with lighter fluid, and set it afire. When the Air Police arrived, Ranger officers were doing a war dance around the flaming blues. The only thing that saved Tucker was that also in the war dance was the one-star assistant commander of the USAF Special Operations Wing at Hurlburt field.

PARASAILING TUCKER'S WAY

Tucker was a sky diver. He lived to get up to 15,000 feet and dive out the door of an airplane, flying like a bird until he opened his parachute. On one occasion, he had a total malfunction over Field 6. Rangers on the ground watched in horror until he opened his reserve parachute low to the ground. One day, he was extolling the virtues of his new Para-commander parachute to two of his captains. The Para-commander is the same kind of parachute that is now pulled behind boats at the beach. In fact, Tucker had already done some parasailing behind a Volkswagen driven down the runway at Field 6.

One afternoon over a beer at the club, Tucker said, "You know, I believe I could get my motorcycle up to 60 miles per hour, pull that 'chute, and sail away, right up in the air."

The two captains who were with him just looked at each other, nodded and shrugged.

"Let's try it!" cried Tucker.

He put his new parachute on, strapped on his motorcycle helmet, and mounted his motorcycle.

"What I want you two guys to do," he told Captains Clark Welch* and Frank Duncan, "is to ride along side of me and grab the handlebars of my motorcycle when I pop the 'chute."

The brilliant trio then rode to the end of the Field 6 runway, lined up abreast with one of the captains on each side of Tucker, and took off down the airstrip. When his speedometer hit 60 MPH, Tucker pulled his ripcord. The Para-commander deployed properly and lifted Tucker from the seat—about three feet off the seat. Tucker then went ass-over-teakettle, bouncing down the runway. The captains, holding his motorcycle upright, slowed to a stop and looked back. Scuffed and bruised, Tucker stood up and yelled, "Well, that didn't work, did it?"

*Clark Welch, as a first lieutenant, was commanding D Company, 2nd Battalion, 28th Infantry on 17 October, 1967 during the Battle on Ong Thanh. He was wounded five times and later was awarded the Distinguished Service Cross. A field is dedicated to him at Camp Rudder, Eglin Air Force Base, Florida (the Florida Ranger Camp).

THE COLONEL'S WIFE

As I said earlier, when I arrived at the Florida Ranger Camp in August of 1968, I had served under four battalion commanders—two in the 82nd Airborne and two in Vietnam. They were all old. All of them had gray hair, and all of them had wives who looked as old as they did.

One day, one of the captains asked me, "Have you met the colonel's wife?"

"No," I answered, "What's she like?"

I was soon to find out.

When I first met Lorraine, I couldn't believe it. Not only was she not old, she was beautiful. Not only was she beautiful, she was poised, confident, gracious, elegant and hospitable. Lorraine is from Columbus, Mississippi, and was raised in the bosom of the old south and steeped in traditional southern manners and traditions.

There are several kinds of southern accents. First, there is the redneck, cornpone nasal twang of Tennessee, Southwest Virginia, Kentucky, Alabama, and north Georgia. There is the blend of linguistic influences that make up the Louisiana dialect, there is the rough-cut Texas/southwest accent, and there is the melodious and smooth accent of Tidewater Virginia and Coastal Carolina. Then there are the marvelous, aristocratic, and syrupy tones of Mississippi. When Lorraine spoke, you could shut your eyes and see the full moon shining through Spanish moss and smell the honeysuckle vines on a barbed wire fence. People would often stand around her just to listen to her talk. Everyone was instantly in love with Lorraine.

In 1991, I was watching a PBS special about the Civil War. Ken Burns was interviewing Shelby Foote, one of the most famous, knowledgeable, and prolific writers about the War Between the States. As Mr. Foote, who was from Mississippi, spoke, I recognized the silky elegance of his accent and immediately thought of Lorraine.

At social functions, the men would gather around Tucker and talk Army, while Lorraine would hold court with the ladies and talk about army moves, babies, pets, and relatives.

The officers' ladies would often gather for teas, luncheons, wine tastings, and baby showers. At these events, Lorraine would invariably be in the center of a giggling mass of bouffant hair and flowered sun dresses. Lorraine had no favorites, she loved all the same and treated everyone equally. She cared mainly about two things: animals and family. She always asked about pets and loved to tell stories about her cats and dogs—and her skunk. If a new wife entered the group and spoke with a southern accent, Lorraine would always ask, "Now, who're yore people?" She believed all southern families are connected in some way, and she wanted to know where the newcomer fit in. She never got around to asking that question to ladies from the north.

According to Kaci Cantrell, wife of Captain Jim Cantrell, Lorraine always stood at the door to say farewell at the end of her social gatherings. As the ladies were departing after one party, Lorraine was saying goodbye to everyone.

"Now, girls," she drawled, "Y'all are all welcome to stop by any time for a visit. I just ask pleeese don't come by on Saterdy mornin' before ten. That's when Tucker will be vacuuming'!"

THE MOTORCYCLE CLUB

One day, a Ranger captain who had just finished a 24-hour walk in the woods grading Ranger students stopped at our camp officers' club for a beer before going home. There was a visiting Air Force captain sitting at the bar. All of a sudden, there was a roar and rapid thumping, then a motorcycle burst through the front door. The rider made a circle around one of the tables, then shot back out the door and thumped back down the steps.

"Who in the hell was that crazy sonuvabitch?" yelled the Air Force captain.

"Oh, that's our commander." The Ranger replied.

THE GREAT
PENSACOLA BIATHLON

"Rangers are supposed to be able to walk long distances," says John Lemoyne, who, as a captain, was Tucker's S-1 (personnel officer) on the Florida Ranger Camp staff. Lemoyne, as a major general (two star), later commanded Fort Benning and then, as a lieutenant general (three star) served as the Army's Deputy Chief of Staff for Personnel.

"Just for the exercise," recalls Lemoyne, "about once a month, I used to walk from my quarters at Eglin Air Force Base to work at the Ranger camp, a distance of about 25 miles. Walking long distances was something Rangers did. I also figured that we as Rangers should know the complete capabilities of the RB-7 rubber boats we were using to teach swamp river navigation to our Ranger students. So I came up with a plan.

"The concept I formed in my mind was to combine forced marching with a long-distance rubber boat trip into a kind of biathlon using two of the skills Rangers used in Florida. We would walk from the camp at Field 6 along the Yellow River Road to where the river empties into Pensacola Bay. We would then paddle an RB-7 across the bay to the Pensacola Naval Base officers' club.

"The walk would be about 20 miles in length and the boat trip would cover about 25 miles, for a combined distance of 45 miles. The purpose of the exercise was just to do it—to test our metal.

"I didn't need to research much about walking, but I needed more information about the boat phase. I talked to fellow Ranger instructor Captain Tom Groppel, who knew about Pensacola Bay, and I talked to a Navy Seal, who advised me concerning the tides and currents and about rubber boats. I also obtained navigational charts to go along with the topographical maps we used in training."

Originally there were to be two boats involved in the operation, but as time grew near, the numbers of Rangers volunteering to make the journey dwindled to nine. That number fit well into an RB-7—four paddlers on each side plus a coxswain in the stern to steer. Lemoyne briefed Tucker on the plan, and of course Tucker volunteered to go along, and so did Groppel. There were some logistics to be worked out. A boat had to be stashed at the terminus of the march, and a van and a truck had to meet the team in Pensacola to haul them and the boat back to the camp.

The team departed Field Six at midnight, and walked at a blistering pace.

"About 15 miles into the march," recalls Tucker, "I knew I had made a big mistake joining the venture. I was a distance runner, so stamina was not a problem, but speed walking, as I had learned in the British commando school, taxed muscles that had not been used in many years. I seized up like a '57 Plymouth with vapor lock!"

But "quit" was not a word that was even in Tucker's vocabulary. The team reached the bay in mid morning, and began the paddling phase.

"Surprisingly, we traveled faster by boat than we did by walking," recalls Lemoyne. "We arrived at the officers club in the afternoon, some 16 hours after starting."

"When we got to the Navy Base," says Tucker, "I was so exhausted the guys had to help me out of the boat."

When Sir Edmond Hillary was asked why he had wanted to climb Mount Everest, he replied, "Because it is there!"

When Captain Mathew Web, the first man to swim the English Channel was asked why he wanted to do it, he said, "Because no one has done it!"

When Tucker was asked why anyone in his right mind would, without having to, want to walk 20 miles, then paddle a small rubber boat across choppy Pensacola Bay, he answered, "I don't know!"

THE WATER TOWER

Tucker kept everyone busy. It seemed that in addition to our normal duties as instructors, we each had a special project that Tucker assigned us. For example, one captain who was injured in a parachute jump, was ordered to write a history of the Florida Ranger Camp. Another was the leader of the camp skydiving team. Others became qualified as scuba divers who came in handy looking for lost weapons in the swamps and rivers. Others were trained as fire fighters.

One day Tucker called me into his office.

"Gross," he said, "you are an artist, right?"

"Yes sir", I answered. "I enjoy painting."

"Good! I want you to paint a Ranger Tab on the water tower."

"That will be a monumental task," I said.

"I don't give a damn as long as you're doing it and I'm not."

"But sir," I argued, "I'm afraid of heights."

He laughed. He knew better than that. We all had undergone mountaineering training in Ranger school, and we routinely rappelled from helicopters and jumped from airplanes.

"Get out of here and get to painting", he ordered.

I made an estimate of the situation and realized I would need help. I enlisted two of my best friends, Captains Jim Cantrell and Frank Duncan. We climbed the 150-foot tower and began work. Painting the black background was easy. It was arranging the letters on the tab was would be difficult. We could not rough in the letters and step back for a look, because we had to climb down the tower, look, make adjustments, then climb back up and move the letters. As a result, I decided to make large paper letters to tape on the tab as a guide. One of the captains stood on the ground and guided me as I moved the letters inches at a time to get them in the correct position. Once it looked right, I taped the letters in place, then outlined them with a yellow grease pencil. I then tore down the paper letters and we began painting. As we painted the yellow letters, we discovered another problem. We couldn't reach the top of the tab while standing on the catwalk that ran around the tower. We solved this by tying off with safety ropes and standing on top of the catwalk rail to paint the top of the tab. Frank Duncan actually rappelled off the top of the tower to put the finishing touches on the very top.

Frank, Jim and I were very pleased when we returned to the camp for a reunion in 2001. The tab was still on the tower. In fact, it lasted until 2009 (38 years) until the Air Force refurbished the tower and painted over it.

Tucker asked the camp commander what it would take to put the Ranger Tab back on the tower. The Air Force said they could have it done for $15,000. I told Tucker he owed Frank, Jim and me some money. We had done it for free.

THE DUCK HUNTER'S HAT

In our day, the one thing that was sacrosanct to all Rangers was the patrol cap. No one else in the Army was authorized to wear it. Rangers wore the cap only during tactical operations. The rest of the time we wore black berets. In fact, the Rangers who parachuted into Grenada were filmed by news crews walking around with their helmets swinging from their harnesses and their patrol caps on their heads.

The patrol cap was Army green in color, with a bendable bill and a soft crown that could be flattened into what was known as the "Ranger Crush". It had felt-lined ear flaps which could be unfolded from inside the cap. It could be rolled up and crammed into jungle fatigue pockets during parachute jumps. Rangers loved their patrol caps. Tucker did not.

Tucker disliked the patrol cap because, he said, it allowed rain water to run down the back of his neck. Forever the innovator, Tucker had a new design for a field cap for the Rangers. He took a camouflaged duck-hunting cap, and sewed a Ranger Tab on it—and wore it to work. He thought it was grand. Every Ranger in the camp thought it was ridiculous.

"A damned duck hunting hat will never grace my head," said Sergeant First Class Jessie L. Stevens, Jr. Everyone agreed. We all lived in fear that Tucker would make us all wear the thing. We didn't want to part with our beloved patrol caps.

Tucker wore the duck hunting cap around for several months, mentioning that he was going to recommend that the Army's uniform board adopt the hat for field wear. No one said anything, but we all laughed at that ridiculous hat on his bald head. Thank God nothing ever came of it.

THE GIN HOLE
LANDING DEATH MARCH

Anyone who knew Tucker knew he was a physical fitness fanatic. He believed that now matter how fit you were, you could always be in better shape. He always believed that the Ranger course was not tough enough, and he constantly thought of ways to make it harder. In 1969, he came up with a real doozy, probably inspired by his experience in the British commando school. It became known as the "Death March".

For several years, the end of the 12-day Field Training Exercise (FTX) that made up the bulk of the training in Florida was an attack by the entire Ranger student company on a simulated Viet Cong bunker system on the banks of the Yellow River at a place marked on the map as Gin Hole Landing. The Vietnam-style village that instructors had built there was realistic to a fault. It had thatched-roof huts, bunkers, tunnels and booby traps. A full company of the 197th Infantry Brigade from Fort Benning was dressed as guerrillas and placed in the village as enemy troops. Demolitions were wired in pits to be set off as the Rangers called for artillery and air strikes. The last attack of Ranger school was a dramatic affair, complete with smoke, Air Force jets, explosions, blank machine-gun fire and a final Ranger assault during which the "guerrillas" played dead or surrendered. Ranger students were then critiqued and loaded on trucks and hauled back to Field 7, where they prepared for graduation.

Tucker thought this was too easy, so he changed the finale. Under Tucker's new scheme of maneuver, Ranger students attacked Gin Hole Landing, were critiqued, and ordered by radio to withdraw to a helicopter pick-up zone. They thought they were going to fly back to Field 7. They were allowed to wait at the PZ until dusk, when they received a radio call telling them that the helicopters had been cancelled and that they would have to walk to Field 7—a distance of 22 kilometers (over 13 miles) away. They were told not to walk on roads or trails. They were to move through the woods in tactical formation. They were told to be at Field 7 by 0800 the next morning for graduation.

I walked the first "Death March". Thankfully, it was a calm clear night with a full moon. Walking through the pine forests in a tactical column was relatively easy. We had to stop when we encountered a road or trail, put out security, and clear the other side before we crossed, which was a time-consuming process. There were lots of sand trails and dirt roads criss-crossing our route. Descending into and crossing thickly vegetated streams was also time-consuming. Still, we made it to camp by 8:00 a.m. as ordered.

Two classes later, I had to walk the Death March again. This time it was a totally dark night with a new moon. Movement through the woods was painfully slow and crossing the juniper thickets near the streams nearly brought us to a halt. By 0500, we were still miles away from camp. I knew I had to have my Ranger platoon at the camp by 0800 so I decided to disobey Tucker's order to move through the woods. I led the platoon to the hard-top road leading from the main Eglin base to the camp. I put the Rangers in a column of twos and told them to move out.

The Ranger students had just endured nine weeks of non-stop training. Most days they had walked at least 18 hours and they were exhausted and emaciated. Now with the end in sight, they were humping down the pavement at a blistering pace, carrying weapons, radios, and rucksacks that probably weighed 50 pounds each. We made it by eight o'clock, but had to wait on two platoons which were running late.

It was tradition for the Rangers to double time past the reviewing stand for graduation. My platoon could hardly walk, much less run. Graduation was a disaster. After the graduation ceremony, medics descended on the new Rangers, many of whom were pouring blood out of their boots.

The next week word got around camp that Tucker had been royally ripped by the Ranger Department Director. When our Ranger graduates got back to Benning, it was said they were too crippled by the Death March to begin Airborne School or take part in other training. Many Rangers returning to their home units allegedly had to take medical leave before resuming their duties.

A common saying among the soldiers who wear the Ranger Tab is, "Ranger School was much harder back when I went through!" The Gin Hole Landing Death March only lasted for three class cycles, but the Rangers who walked it can truthfully say, "It was harder in my day!"

THE FIRE MARSHAL

A month or so after we moved the Ranger camp from Field 7 to Field 6, Captain Clark Welch went to Tucker with a problem. None of the Florida Ranger Camp captains used initiative as did Clark. He was always quick to identify problems and to suggest solutions.

"Sir," he said, "We have no fire protection at the camp. The only time a fire truck shows up is when an aircraft is going to land. We need the capability to fight fires twenty four hours a day."

Clark then explained that before he came in the Army, he had been a volunteer fireman in New Hampshire. He said he had had some training and he would be glad to volunteer to serve as the camp fire marshal.

Tucker agreed and Clark set to work. He tried to talk the Eglin Air Force Base fire chief into giving the camp a fire engine. Of course the Air Force refused. So Clark improvised. He scrounged a long-bed pickup truck, some hoses, extinguishers and some other gear and put together our own small fire truck. He even taught fire-fighting classes to other instructors and soon had a small semi-trained fire department. Clark was proud of the work he had done and Tucker was happy that we had some kind of response at the camp in case we had a fire.

And several months later, it happened. A sergeant ran into Tucker's office shouting, "The Alpha Company equipment room is on fire!"

"Where's Captain Welch?" Tucker asked as he ran toward the burning building.

"Sir, he's gone TDY (temporary duty) to Fort Benning."

"Oh yeah," Tucker remembered. "He went yesterday."

When he arrived at the Alpha Company building, smoke was pouring from the doors and windows. The fire truck was sitting next to the building and everyone assumed it was there to fight the fire.

"Where are the people Welch trained to be firemen?" Tucker asked.

"We're right here," answered several voices.

"Well what are you doing?"

"Well, Sir, It seems that no one can find the keys to the truck. We got some of the extinguishers off, but we can't move the truck."

"Well who the hell has the keys!"

"Sir, I think Captain Welch has them in his pocket."

"You mean the same Captain Welch, our fire marshal, who is TDY at Fort Benning?"

"That's affirm, Sir."

The Alpha Company equipment room burned to the ground.

So did the fire truck.

THE FOREST FIRE

One day during each Ranger cycle, an entire flight school class from Fort Rucker (some 50 helicopters) flew down to Eglin for their final exercise before graduation. This airmobile exercise consisted of flying our Ranger students into simulated combat exactly the way the aviators would have to lift Infantrymen in Vietnam. That day, we had more helicopter lift for 250 Ranger students than any 800-man Infantry battalion ever had in Vietnam. During that day, a variety of intricate airmobile insertions and pick ups were planned to test both our Rangers' tactics and the fledgling pilots' techniques.

On one day, as the choppers were on final approach to a landing zone in the East Bay Swamp, a Ranger instructor popped a smoke grenade to help the pilots gauge wind direction. When the smoke grenade started a small fire in the grass, one of the Ranger students commented to the instructor that maybe they ought to stomp the fire out.

"To hell with the fire! Continue your mission, Ranger", said the instructor.

A short time later, the fire had burned a large circle in the grass on the landing zone. At that time, Tucker showed up in his command-and-control chopper. Tucker remembers landing at the burning field, but instructors on the scene remember the incident differently. They claim that Tucker had his helicopter hover over the fire to attempt to "blow it out". Regardless of whether he simply landed or attempted to blow the fire out, the result was the same. The rotor wash from the Huey blasted burning embers in all directions, quickly spreading the fire. Hours later, the fire had jumped over Highway 98 and was threatening several homes and had burned acre upon acre of Eglin's pine forest. Every fire engine from nearby Hurlburt field, Mary Esther, and Navarre arrived as Ranger students scraped and hacked at the fire with their entrenching tools.

Tucker was heard telling the Ranger captain who had cried, "To hell with the fire" that he was not to come out of the field until every spark of the fire was extinguished. As Tucker's helicopter took off, it churned more burning embers into the air. Just another day of Ranger training.

AN OLD SOLDIER
FINDS PEACE

Tucker is at peace with the world now. He still actively participates in the operation of his marina. One can often find him driving a tractor about the lot, or pulling boats out of the water for repair. His office is in a concrete boat, actually a small ship. Commissioned for the U.S. Army, the *USS Hodgekins*, a 150-foot vessel, was used during the 1920s to ferry soldiers and supplies. Later, during its career, the boat was transformed into a restaurant and belonged to several different owners before Tucker bought it in 1978. He had it towed to its present location in his marina. Over the years, the old boat was rocked by hurricanes and sometimes the deck slanted so badly that one could hardly walk on it. It has since been stabilized and now serves as The Boat Marina's offices as well as a great place to entertain.

Besides repairing boats, Tucker enjoys taking care of his birds and fish. The marina is a wildlife refuge with ducks, geese, gulls, great blue herons, pelicans, and peacocks wandering about, and a school of hungry fish that lives in the shallow waters next to the old boat. Occasionally he still finds a battle to fight. His eight years as a member of the Fort Walton Beach City Council gave him many opportunities to do battle, and he never hesitates to dash off a letter to the editor about a favorite cause. But now, he mostly enjoys sitting in his office at The Boat Marina visiting old comrades and sharing his thoughts and insights with friends. There is a non-stop parade of old soldiers and local business people stopping by to pay homage, simply visit, or drink his gin. His Ranger instructors from the time he commanded the Florida Ranger Camp stay in touch and call or visit him often. Each year, he attends the Ranger Ball thrown by the 6th Ranger Training Battalion, where he insures that no young Ranger has to buy his own drinks.

Tucker has settled into the life of a beach local. Every day at 11:00, he goes to lunch, not at some fast food joint or fern bar. He seeks out the mom-and-pop restaurants that have been in town for years, where he knows and supports the owners. He always takes a to-go box back to the boat to feed his fish and birds. He and Lorraine still love to meet at the yacht club for an early dinner at least once a week.

Tucker's span of influence has been amazing over the years considering the fact that he retired as a lieutenant colonel. He seemingly knows every general officer who served during his time, and he stays in contact with many of them. In fact, while I was visiting him a few months ago, Retired Air Force (four-star) General Chuck Horner, the air component commander during the first Gulf War, walked in with his wife, Mary Jo, and spent an afternoon with Tucker, talking about everything from cooking to the Afghanistan War.

In 2001, Tucker had a three-story tower with a deck on top built adjacent to the old boat. He says he climbs up in the evenings to watch the sunset, to meditate, and sometimes cry. Though he is still a soldier at heart, he has spent more years at his marina than he spent in the Army. He is part of that place now. He says that when he dies, he wants to be cremated and he wants his ashes mixed with cement, and poured into the keel of the old Boat.

LIEUTENANT COLONEL (RETIRED) JAMES M. TUCKER'S AWARDS AND DECORATIONS

Silver Star (The nation's third highest decoration for gallantry in action)
Distinguished Flying Cross
Bronze Star Medal with "V" device for valor and two Oak Leaf Clusters
Air Medal with three Oak Leaf Clusters
Soldier's Medal (The Army's highest peacetime award for heroism)
Meritorious Service Medal
Army Commendation Medal with "V" device for valor
and one Oak Leaf Cluster
Purple Heart with one Oak Leaf Cluster
Combat Infantryman's Badge
Expert Infantryman's Badge
Senior Parachutist Badge
British Commando Medal

and of course, the Ranger Tab

Tucker with BG Leroy Manor, USAF Special Operations Wing

Tucker at his going-away party with C Co, 1-15 Inf troops in Germany

Tucker greets Secretary of the Army Stanley Resor

Tucker and BG Sidney Berry on a boat in the Yellow River

General Richard Cavazos

Promotion to major

Costume party

Lorraine

General Hugh Shelton

Florida Ranger Camp circa 1970

Right to Left: Cpt John Lemoyne, Cpt Jim Cantrell and an
unidentified Ranger brief a British General

General Richard Cavazos

Pappy White is between Cpt Dick White and Tucker with members
of the US Army Ranger Association

Cpts John Gross, Frank Duncan, and Jim Cantrell on the water tower

Lt. James M. Tucker —
Congratulations on your Dariry deed,
and best wishes :
Paul Freeman

Soldiers Medal Jan, 1960 Ft Benning, GA

Tucker receives the Soldiers' Medal from MG Paul Freeman

Lorraine, Carlton, Tucker, Twink the cat, and Fay the boxer

Lorraine, Carlton and Fay meet Tucker and his rifle company
after a 200-mile road march

Tucker as a cadet at the Citadel

Clark Welch receives the Distinguished Service Cross from
LTG John Lemoyne. Lacey Welch looks on

Cpt Clark Welch receives a Bronze Star at a
Ranger graduation at Field Seven

From left to right: Cpt Frank Duncan, Cpt George Utter, Tucker, General
Aubrey S. Newman, Maj Bob Frix, Maj Jim Shelton, Cpt Clark Welch

Mr.Clean—Tucker in his prime

Carlton Tucker
1960-1998

Lorraine and grand children Kaye, Carlton, Collier, and Hampton

Lieutenant Colonel John Gross